Community Leisure and

Community Leisure and Recreation

Theory and practice

Edited by Les Haywood

Butterworth-Heinemann Ltd
Linacre House, Jordan Hill, Oxford OX2 8DP

℞ A member of the Reed Elsevier plc group

OXFORD LONDON BOSTON
MUNICH NEW DELHI SINGAPORE SYDNEY
TOKYO TORONTO WELLINGTON

First published 1994

British Library Cataloguing in Publication Data
Community Leisure and Recreation: Theory and practice
  I. Haywood, Les
  306.4

ISBN 0 7506 0688 6

306.4812 /

Printed in Great Britain by Biddles Ltd, Guildford and King's Lynn

Contents

Contributors

Norman Borrett is Principal Lecturer in Community Studies at Bradford and Ilkley Community College where he teaches on a range of community recreation and management courses at undergraduate and masters levels. He is Editor of *Leisure Services UK* (1991).

Peter Bramham is Senior Lecturer in Leisure Studies at the Leeds Metropolitan University. He has written extensively on leisure policy and politics, most recently contributing to the comparative texts *Leisure and Urban Processes* (1989) and *Leisure Policies in Europe* (1993).

Hugh Butcher was a social worker and community worker and has taught sociology, social policy and community practice at a number of universities and colleges in the UK. He is currently Head of Department of Applied and Community Studies at Bradford and Ilkley Community College.

John Capenerhurst is a Lecturer in Leisure Studies at Bradford and Ilkley Community College and the Metropolitan University of Leeds. He is co-author of *Understanding Leisure* and has written a number of articles on community leisure and tourism.

Les Haywood is a freelance lecturer and writer. He was formerly Head of Community Leisure Studies at Bradford and Ilkley Community College and is co-author of *Understanding Leisure.*

Maurice Mullard is a Principal Lecturer in Economics and Politics. He has written *The Politics of Public Expenditure*, now in its second edition, and *Understanding Economic Policy*. He is also co-author of *Thatcherism and Local Government.*

Preface

The book is organized in two parts – Part One (Theoretical Dimensions) and Part Two (Practical Applications) each containing three chapters. Part One begins with Hugh Butcher's discussion of 'The concept of community practice', in which he initially describes the recent growth in the use of the term 'community' in order to characterize contemporary approaches to decision-making and service-delivery in a range of public services such as health, education and recreation. He goes on to examine critically the concept of community practice in order to identify its defining characteristics and historical development, and then proceeds to scrutinize the legitimacy of the claims of public services to have adopted a genuine community approach as an alternative to orthodox 'provider-led', professionalized and bureaucratic models. The chapter concludes by reviewing systematically the claims made for the community-practice-based approach, distinguishing 'instrumental' claims, like resource efficiency and effectiveness in meeting client needs from 'value' claims, such as the growth in social solidarity, democratic control and the empowerment of individuals and community groups.

In Chapter 2 Les Haywood draws on the concept of community practice outlined in Chapter 1 in exploring the nature of community leisure and recreation, beginning with an analysis of the definitive characteristics of community recreation – focus on specific groups, devolution and localism, community development and an integrated approach to service provision. He then reviews critically the range of methods of community-orientated leisure service delivery which has been developed by local authorities and other public agencies such as the sports councils, and by voluntary bodies. The author then discusses the implications for the management of a community-practice approach, focusing initially on the need to perceive the community as a resource and to devolve power and responsibilities. Finally, the author stresses the necessity to reappraise the very nature of professional recreation management practice and the fundamental form of the activities promoted and developed as community leisure and recreation.

Chapter 3 examines the wider political and economic contexts in which contemporary community practice approaches to the provision of leisure and recreation are situated. The authors, Maurice Mullard and Norman Borrett, begin by outlining the current political dominance of market liberal economics in Western countries, and their recent growth in former command economies of Easter Europe. They then proceed to explain the key concepts and values that constitute a market liberal approach, and discuss the implications of market liberal economics for the provision of public services. The authors conclude with a number of case studies examining aspects of countryside recreation, broadcasting and local authority recreation as a means of exemplifying the workings of market liberalism in the public provision of leisure.

Part Two contains discussions of the application of community practice approaches to three areas of leisure and recreation practice and provision – the arts, sports and physical recreation, and tourism. Chapter 4 'Community arts' written by Peter Bramham, examines the nature of community arts and the characteristics that distinguish this approach from traditional arts, emphasizing localism, active participation, innovation and ease of access. He then discusses recent historical developments, focusing on the role of community arts within the Arts Council of Great Britain and the policies and politics of arts funding. Having thus established the conceptual and institutional frameworks for community arts, the author proceeds into a critical account of their contemporary significance in terms of social policy, urban politics, and citizenship and participation, and concludes by considering their role in the increasingly market liberal orientated local economies of the 1990s.

Chapter 5, 'Community sports and physical recreation', opens with an analysis of the ways in which 'community sports' may differ from traditional sports, focusing on comparisons of aims and objectives and the nature and structure of sports forms, and on issues such as attitudes to gender, race and cultural pluralism, violence and deviant sports behaviour, and elitism and professionalism. The author, Les Haywood, then examines community sport and physical recreation in practice in order to determine the extent to which initiatives adopting an overtly 'community' stance, such as local authority schemes, the Sports Council's Action Sports programmes, and Football in the Community meet the criteria specified for a community-practice approach outlined in the first part of this chapter, and in Chapters 1 and 2.

Chapter 6, by John Capenerhurst, analyses the concept of community tourism. After an initial discussion of the nature of tourism in its broad sense, the author identifies two elements that are of particular significance in defining a community approach. The first of these is the issue of local community control over the development of tourism and includes an analysis of the impacts of tourism on communities at different spatial levels, together with discussions of case studies of community participation in planning tourism-development strategies in Canada and the UK. The second element is that of collective provision for tourism, which is discussed in a European context. The centralized provision in the former soviet Union and its Eastern

European satellites, aimed at the workforce as a whole, is contrasted with the notion of subsidized holidays as a social need for disadvantaged groups in the market economies of the West. The chapter concludes with a consideration of the possible role for community tourism in economies dominated by market liberal policies.

Les Haywood

Acknowledgements

The authors acknowledge, with thanks, permission to include excerpts from articles originally published as follows: 'The 'Community Practice' approach to local public service provision' by Hugh Butcher in the *Community Development Journal*, (1986), Vol. 21, No. 2, Oxford University Press; 'Policy developments in Community Leisure and Recreation' by Les Haywood and Ian Henry in *Leisure Management* (July and August 1986); and 'Social Tourism' by John Capenerhurst in Kew, F. (Ed.) (1989) *Into the 1990's*, Bradford and Ilkley Community College.

The editor wishes to express his gratitude to his colleagues Hugh Butcher, Maurice Mullard, Norman Borrett, Peter Bramham and John Capenerhurst for their contributions to the development and production of this text. Special thanks are also due to Peter Bramham for his help with preparation of the final manuscript, and to Dr Ian Henry of Loughborough University for his help with the original development of ideas on the 'Concept of community recreation' included in Chapter 2 of this book.

Part One

Theoretical Dimensions

The concept of community practice

Hugh Butcher

Community practice constitutes part of a distinctive, yet relatively undeveloped, approach to decision-making and service-delivery within a range of UK public services. The approach – of which community recreation and leisure is a part – is fairly new, and in many ways represents an alternative to, and embraces a critique of, more orthodox and well established approaches to policy and service provision within the public sector.

The range of occupations and services that have sought to apply the community practice approach is large, and expanding. Some, like community care, community education and community policing, have become quite well established; others, like community health, community development, community business, and community youth work, are of more recent origin. Scarcely a month goes by without additions being made to the growing list of community policies, programmes and initiatives, and the avid collector of new varieties will have found, since the mid-1980s, references to community probation (Henderson, 1991), community radio (Community Radio Association, 1986), and community architecture (Wates and Knevitt, 1987). There have even been apparently serious references to 'community pharmacy' and 'community prisons'. In one interesting study Peter Willmott (1989) surveyed examples of five approaches to community practice in some detail (including local government decentralization, and community policing) and provided the reader with briefer portraits of eight others (including community arts and community social work). In another overview David Donnison (1989) touched on a still wider range of projects and initiatives which he saw as exemplifying what he called the 'community-based approach' – including neighbourhood councils, housing co-operatives, and youth projects.

Such growth and diversity prompts the question – do these exemplars of the community practice approach have anything in common and, indeed, do they have any real substance? Perhaps only the prefix ('community') itself is important. Sceptics have noted on more than one occasion that 'community' tends to get applied as a kind of 'spray-on' word, deployed to lend legitimacy and positive feelings to a variety of otherwise very diverse and maybe, in the end, not particularly new and innovative practices and approaches. Community, the argument goes, is one of those words – like 'democracy' and 'freedom' – that few can really disagree with and so to apply the tag to a particular policy or initiative may serve to lend it credence and acceptability (Plant *et al.*, 1980).

A text on community approaches to recreation and leisure thus possibly suffers from a built-in handicap – namely a legitimate uncertainty among its readers concerning the authenticity, or even very existence, of such an approach. In a sense this question constitutes a major sub-theme of this book as a whole, but in this opening chapter we address the issues head on. We begin by exploring how the community-practice approach differs from more traditional models of public-service provision and seek to situate its growth in an historical context. We then seek to clarify some of the central terms to be used in the critical analysis of such an approach – showing how 'community' *can* be used with precision in policy analysis, and then explore the meanings of a number of related terms of central importance to this book, e.g. those of 'community practice' and 'community policy'. Finally, we review in general terms both the claims made on behalf of the community approach, and also note some of the limitations, reservations and worries that have been expressed about such an approach.

As the central concern of this chapter is with conceptual clarification, it may be useful to offer a preliminary definition of community practice without further ado. The approach requires:

- Viewing clients and public as co-participants in the determination of import aspects of service provision.
- Tackling problems and decision-making on a collective rather than an individual basis.
- Recognizing the value of indigenous community resources in the promotion and delivery of services designed to meet need.
- Awareness of cultural diversity in definitions of 'need', and a recognition of the importance of planning and delivering services in a culturally sensitive and responsive way.
- Commitment to meeting the needs of disadvantaged people and groups as a priority.

Community practice and the challenge to the orthodox model of public-service provision

What might be called the established or orthodox model of local public policy-making and service-delivery has come in for considerable criticism over recent years and such criticism has helped to define its central features more clearly. Hoggett and Hambleton (1987) have labelled it the 'Bureau-Paternalist' model, Keane (1988) has called it 'State-Administered Socialism' and Croft and Beresford (1992) talk of the

'Provider-Led' model. We will adopt the term 'bureau-professional model' as a straightforward and neutral description of this orthodox model.

This bureau-professional model reached its fullest expression within, and enjoyed a relatively good 'fit' with, the institutions and practices of what has become known as the 'post-war settlement', i.e. the mixture of Keynsian demand management of a mixed economy (with significant levels of social ownership), of Beveridge-style welfare statism underpinning a range of social citizenship rights, and a representative –electoral form of political democracy predicated on modest public participation between elections and virtually none in arenas other than the strictly governmental. Public policy and administration in those arenas in which the state interfaced directly with the public, e.g. housing, personal social services, policing, health provision, and even local democracy itself, came to embrace certain common assumptions during the period 1945–75:

- Centralized, top-down planning and decision-making.
- Clear separation of policy-making from service administration and practice.
- Large-scale bureaucratic organization and control of service-delivery.
- High levels of professional influence and power, even hegemony, in policy execution.
- The 'user' of services as an individual consumer.
- An emphasis upon standardized provision for reasons of fairness, economy and control.

Nowhere were these features more clearly seen to develop over the post-war period than in local government, reaching their fullest expression in the 1974 reorganization of municipal government into vast bureaucratic systems seen, at the time, as the best response to tackling large and daunting urban problems. This model has come in for criticism from all points of the political spectrum, and it seems that those criticisms have gained force as confidence in the framing assumptions of the post-war settlement – Keynsianism, public ownership, Beveridgian welfare, and electoral democracy – have been progressively undermined.

The idea of a 'post-war settlement' is of course a construct born of hindsight, and the rather glib use of generalizations about a 30-year period of what was, after all, a time of rapid social and economic change in UK society is bound to be rather superficial, and therefore questionable. Nevertheless the early 1970s do represent a significant historical turning point, one in which taken-for-granted assumptions were questioned and radical new thinking given the opportunity to germinate and take root. The reasons for this sea-change in policy assumptions and practice have been much debated (see Mishra, 1984), though there is little doubt that a significant triggering factor was the 1973 world oil crisis, during which major Middle-Eastern oil producers, operating through the OPEC cartel, demanded a fourfold increase in oil prices, thereby nudging the UK and other industrial, oil-dependent countries in Western Europe into major economic recession. That economic crisis has had multiple and far-reaching consequences (see Gamble, 1988), not least of which of course has been the resurgence of New Right principles, prescriptions and policies, defined and adapted to address the difficulties of the new age.

The New Right has been underpinned by a combination of two sets of political and economic theory – economic liberalism, which celebrates the virtues of free market competition and possessive individualism; and social and moral conservatism, with its belief in family, civic responsibility and nationhood. It has offered its own trenchant and far-reaching critique of public-sector services, with their attendant bureaucracy and 'nannying' paternalism. The New Right has ushered in attempts to roll back the state, to expose a reduced public sector to the rigours of market discipline, and to enhance freedoms through expansion of individual consumer choice.

It is within this climate of change and critique that the community-practice model has also found space to develop and take root. It too offers a sustained critique of the bureau-professional model, and it too advocates principles, programmes and practices deemed appropriate to the economic, political and social realities of late twentieth-century UK society.

Deficiencies in the bureau-professional model

The perceived deficiencies of the bureau-professional model, drawing on both New Right critiques and the reservations expressed by advocates of the community-practice alternative, seem to cluster under three main heads, and may be summarized as follows.

Organizational failure and 'bureaucratic crisis'

The bureau-professional model:

- Fails adequately to meet certain needs, e.g. those of minorities, women, the unemployed, etc., a problem that increases as society becomes increasingly diverse and pluralistic.
- Fails to innovate, and to keep pace with increasingly rapid change in society as a whole (whether the result of new technologies, demographic change, 'Europeanization' and so forth). It does not encourage experimentation and risk-taking, and can suffer from a kind of bureaucratic inertia and conservatism.
- Fails to secure joint planning, and integrated

service-delivery. Social needs, e.g. for social care, often don't 'fit' functional organizational and professional specialisms. Large bureaucracies and established professional groups are protective of their 'territory' and the consumer can suffer.

Political failure and 'legitimation crisis'

The bureau-professional model:

- Promotes centralized decision-making, which locks people out from having a voice and influence in day-to-day decision-making. Protest movements, and possibly illegal action by those who feel their demands have been forgotten or ignored, may result.
- Systematically differentiates 'politics' from 'administration'. Users and voters are distanced from their political representatives, and a kind of 'democratic deficit' results.

Resource difficulties and 'fiscal crisis'

The bureau-professional model:

- Tends to emphasize 'producer' interests at the expense of service-user interests, e.g. the educational 'establishment' at the expense of parents and pupils; and professional social workers at the expense of their clients.

- Increasing public expenditure on welfare and other services is 'needs'-driven and seems, in theory, infinitely expandable: the increasing burden of taxation to support such expansion, it is said, ultimately saps and hobbles the economically 'productive' areas of society and can evoke a fiscal crisis.

The community-practice model of public policy and service provision

In Tables 1.1 and 1.2 the distinctive features of the community-practice model are identified, and contrasted with those of the bureau-professional model. Table 1.1 focuses upon policy and organizational distinctions, and Table 2.2 on aspects that relate to professional practice and service delivery.

Comparing the two models highlights the key features of the community-practice approach. These features will be illustrated and discussed further in later chapters, but for now we shall concentrate on underlining, and discussing further, three particular characteristics of the model:

- The role of the public and service user in policy and practice processes.
- The conceptions of community embraced within the model.
- The practice skills and perspectives employed by professional workers who operate within the community-practice framework.

The public as active participant

It is clear from Tables 1.1 and 1.2 that the public – in the general sense, and specifically as service-users – have a more active role in all stages of the policy and delivery process within the community-practice model than in the bureau-professional model. The community-practice model is intended to facilitate and enhance the ability of members of the public to achieve a greater voice in decision-making processes (via direct user and community participation in management and consultative processes, committees and forums, 'going local' and devolved management schemes, etc.), as well as encouraging significant participation by actual and potential users in the delivery of services (as members

Table 1.1 The differences in policy and organization between the community–practice and bureau–professional models

The 'bureau-professional' model of public policy and service delivery	*The 'community-practice' model of public policy and service delivery*
Emphasis on centralized decision-making and policy control	Emphasis on devolved/decentralized decision-making and policy control
Democratic/public influence exercised at 'arm's length' via representative democracy (limited public/ consumer involvement in decision-making)	Democratic/public influence exercised via mixture of representative and direct democracy (more extensive public/consumer involvement in decision-making)
Clear distinction drawn between 'policy' and management	Distinction between 'policy' and 'management' blurred
Tendency to uniform, standardized conception of consumer 'need'; 'fairness' ensured by treating people equally; efficiency via economies of scale of standard provision	Tendency to pluralistic conception of consumer 'need'; fairness obtained by treating people equitably; efficiency by more sensitive matching of service to need
Hierarchical management (top-down – clear, simple lines of accountability and responsibility. Operational decisions typically drawn to higher levels	Devolved management and accountability. Operational decisions pushed down to lowest possible level
Organizational control emphasizes structure (bureaucracy)	Organizational control emphasizes values (culture)
'Vertical' communications emphasized, roles and structures well defined	'Horizontal' communications emphasized, roles and structures more fluid
'Departmental' and professional specialisms emphasized	'Holistic' emphasis – interdependence between professional and organizational specialisms

Table 1.2 The differences in practice and delivery between the
community–practice and bureau-professional models

The bureau-professional model of public policy and service delivery	*The community-practice model of public policy and service delivery*
Workers' expertise deployed to identify needs according to established prof./admin. criteria, and to make provision in terms of predetermined policies	Workers' expertise deployed to assist communities to articulate needs/demands and to resource solutions; develops in partnership with community
Worker structures the worker/client relationship; clear separation of roles (method is 'participant dependent'). 'Top-down' process of problem-solving	Worker is 'on tap' rather than 'on top'; some blurring of roles (method is 'participant independent'). Interactive/partnership model of problem-solving
'Provider' skills and professional expertise emphasized, e.g. fact-gathering, planning, delivering	Enabling and facilitative skills are emphasized, e.g. groupwork, communication
Bulk of work is with individuals, or 'aggregates' of individuals, as clients and consumers	Bulk of work is with communities (individuals being regarded as members of community organizations that represent members' interests). 'Users' and 'citizens' rather than clients and consumers

of self-managed and resourced action groups, voluntary organizations, clubs and so forth). Pluralistic conceptions of need and reduction of departmental and professional boundaries and specialisms also favour a more public and consumer responsive approach to service provision.

The community dimension

Community is a notoriously slippery concept, as likely to be used as a 'hurrah' word to legitimate and approve, as to be employed in a strictly descriptive or analytical sense. And yet the word is used to define the very model of policy and practice that is the focus of our concerns in this book. So we must clearly offer some conceptual clarification.

Two senses of 'community' have been hinted at – as a value term and as a descriptive term. When we deploy the word in its descriptive sense we are using the social scientists' meaning of the concept, to refer to a group or network of people who share something in common. When, as in Table 1.2, we note that the community-practice approach calls for a focus on work with communities (or with individuals as *members* of a community), we are using this meaning of the term.

Etymological explanations of the origin of 'community' points to 'having something in common' as its root, and that 'something in common' generally refers to either the characteristics of the network itself, e.g. to the type or level of interaction that exists between members, or the people who make it up (common ethnicity, religion, culture, etc.). The two often go hand in hand; shared culture promotes social interaction, which, in turn, reinforces a sense of cultural identity.

This descriptive, social-scientific use of the term thus yokes together social and psychological referents. Members of communities are *interrelated* as part of a social network and they *recognize* themselves as part of that network. Peter Willmott's (1989) use of the idea of the 'community of attachment' is helpful here, because it conveys the twin notion of 'being part of' in a sociological sense and 'identifying with' in a psychological sense.

Communities of attachment are conventionally viewed as being of two types – territorial, where the attachment is to place (neighbourhood, village, estate), and interest, where the basis of attachment derives from characteristics *other* than physical proximity, e.g. occupation, religion, ethnicity. When reference is made to community policies and initiatives, it is possible that the 'community' is being used in its descriptive sense only, to refer to territorial site or social location of the initiative. Community care *may* mean no more and no less than organizational support services for people in their home locality rather than in an institution.

Quite often, though, the policies and practices that carry the community tag are put forward as embracing something *qualitatively* different, as embodying and/or realizing *values* that are not to be found in more orthodox 'bureau-professional' approaches. Being precise and clear about what these values are is far from easy, and in another publication we have sought to derive them from a particular view of the individual in society known as 'communitarianism' (Butcher *et al.*, forthcoming). For our purposes here it is sufficient to identify three clusters of values, already signalled in Tables 1.1 and 1.2, which seem to comprise the normative dimension of community. These are:

- A positive value placed on participative activity undertaken with others: the sense of common goals and purposes, of playing a part in, and contribution to, the collective life of the group.
- A positive value placed on friendship, support and mutuality deriving from the element of social solidarity characteristic of community.
- The positive value of locating oneself in a framework of understandings and meanings that helps to make sense of one's world, and one's place in it.

Community, as value, is in other words a celebration of connectedness, through a 'sense' of membership, through shared activity and decision-making, and through a shared understanding of the world.

It is this interpretation of community, with its emphasis on sharing, connectedness and social solidarity,
that provokes a particular sort of criticism, that 'community' is a fraudulent concept, one based on ideal-
ized and unrealistic notions of harmony and
consensus. If community ever existed like this (and,
so the argument goes, it probably never did), then it
certainly doesn't, and cannot, take this form in modern societies riven by conflicting sectional interests
stemming from economic, religious, ethnic, occupa-
tional, gender, and a host of other individual and
social differences.

Such a criticism is, however, misplaced. First, to
experience conflict in one social context does not
mean that, in another context, one may not experience a sense of attachment and belonging. It may well
be the case, in a general historical sense, that levels of
attachment (and therefore of community in its various guises) have been attenuated through the growth
of conflictual and competitive relationships in society.
However, it is by no means clear that these types of
social relation always vary in inverse ratio (*inter*-
group conflicts *can* serve to increase *intra*-group solidarity) and, in any event, research evidence shows
that communities of attachment do exist on a widespread scale in contemporary Britain (Willmott, 1986).

Second, of course, the normative use of community
addresses these reservations in a somewhat different
way. Here, the argument is a prescriptive one – that
the impact of contemporary trends on 'community' is
negative, and something to be deplored, and that
attention must be given to neutralizing or reversing
the impact of such trends.

The real difficult stems from the conflation of the two
meanings of community, a failure to distinguish fact
from value. This can happen when policy-makers
develop and promote policies that *assume* the exis-

tence of (strong, widespread) community networks without first of all verifying the truth of such assumptions. It is possible, in other words, to embrace community as value, e.g. to believe it preferable that physically disabled or mentally handicapped people are better cared for in the community than in large institutions, only to find that, under particular circumstances, policies based on a community-practice approach don't work (because, for example, particular inner-city areas or peripheral housing estates have rapidly changing, or otherwise distinctive, characteristics).

Practice skills and perspectives

The elaboration of the community-practice model in Table 1.2 also provides a summary of the professional roles, skills and perspectives required to implement this particular approach. It amounts to the adoption of a 'community development' (AMA,1989) way of working. The professional worker seeks to forge a 'partnership' between agency and community whereby she/he can offer help in the identification of needs, and formulation of plans, The worker then seeks to assist the community or, more accurately, its representative organizations, to gain access to the agencies' resources in a way that is most effective in meeting its identified needs and demands. The community ideally moves from passive client or 'user' of services to that of being a user and citizen, responsible for negotiating a particular package of resources designed to meet a self-defined need. The professional worker, and his/her organization, is 'on tap', and the worker uses inter-personal, group work and communication skills (as well as, of course, technical skills and knowledge) to assist the community achieve the best fit between need and resources.

Claims and rationales, weaknesses and worries

So far we have only touched on the supposed benefits of the community-practice approach in tangential ways. For example, in the previous section we noted that it is seen by some to embrace values that are qualitatively different to those found in more orthodox bureau-professional approaches. In the section before that it was suggested that the search for alternatives to the orthodox model stemmed from an increasing awareness of the deficiencies (effectiveness, costliness, etc.) of that model, of its inability to deliver effective services in a changed society. We are now in a position to examine, in an explicit and direct way, the 'case' made for the community-practice approach. This seems to rest on two broad types of claim: 'instrumental' ones, e.g. that such practice is either more effective or resource-efficient than alternatives; and 'value' claims, that such practice advances social goals like social responsibility and independence, or contributes to the development of a more democratic society, with citizens 'empowered' to play a more active part in determining the conditions of their own lives, and of their society more generally.

Resource efficiency

The argument on resource efficiency grounds has, not unexpectedly in a time of public expenditure cutbacks and resource constraints, been a popular one. Within the community-education movement a central theme has been the need to deploy expensive educational plant and facilities for the benefit of the community as a whole. Making available community school facilities for evening, weekend and vacation use not only helps to recast the concept of education as a lifelong process and enables the school to become a focus for community action and community development, it also makes for a more effective use of valuable campus facilities. Arguments about resources have also been an important component in debates concerning community care. Walker (1982) points out that the proposed expansion of community care in the 1960s was manifestly economic. The desire to reduce the costs of replacing the large number of Victorian mental hospitals and other institutions nearing obsolescence was a critical factor in winning support for the concept. Cheaper still would be care by the community and, from the mid-1970s, as public-expenditure constraints tightened (and the predicted expansion in number of the very elderly came ever closer), so the significance of the informal sector in matters of social care was increasingly invoked in official statement and policy research.

Cheapness and resource-efficiency are not of course necessarily the same thing. The implementation of community-practice strategies may well provide for a more efficient deployment of school plant and facilities, or release an increase in support available to vulnerable members of the community, but increased resources will probably be necessary to generate such benefits (Hadley and McGrath, 1984). Without additional resource inputs, attempts to implement community-practice approaches must be viewed suspiciously; as a 'tokenistic' strategy designed to offload welfare-state responsibilities on to an ill-supported community (a form of negative discrimination against poor and disadvantaged areas, and against women as primary carers within the informal sector).

Effectiveness

The argument that community-orientated provision represents a more effective method of meeting agency objectives has also been put forward in a number of contexts. Community 'treatment' of offenders and community 'care' of dependants is seen to avoid the worst effects of institutionalization associated with psychiatric hospitals and custodial institutions.

Community youth work and community social work are also deemed to be more effective because interventions are likely to be more coherent and relevant – stemming from the fact that community practice encourages the youth worker and social worker to become more accessible to potential clients, to develop greater knowledge of local needs and resources, and to undertake more preventative work.

Such claims remain to be thoroughly tested. Although a number of exploratory studies along such lines have been undertaken (Hadley and McGrath, 1984; Wallis and Mee, 1983) a thoroughgoing appraisal of 'effectiveness' arguments remains to be carried out. In any event, questions of effectiveness can rarely be tested through straightforward comparisons between the outcomes of orthodox and community-practice approaches to service delivery. Claims made for the effectiveness of community practice are often couched, and therefore must be evaluated, in terms of *divergent* sets of outcomes. Identifying and clarifying the aims and values that lie behind the pursuit of such outcomes thus becomes a prerequisite to sound evaluation.

Family and personal responsibility

Arguments for 'community practice' that are grounded in particular *value* positions are more easily identified with established positions on the political spectrum, and are supported by specific views concerning the role of public services, and of the relation between state agencies and the public served. For some, the advocacy of community practice is couched in terms of enhancing social responsibility, increasing community solidarity and coherence, and promoting the development of voluntary associations as a bulwark and alternative to state provision. Community treatment of offenders may, for example, be preferable to custodial methods if it encourages the offender to support his or her dependants through normal work, if it promotes a constructive use of leisure time, and if, via the development of new interests, it leads to reappraisal of self-image and hence more responsible social attitudes and behaviour (Adams, 1981).

Community approaches to social work, youth work, and other services may equally be viewed as important elements in a pluralist strategy designed to overcome the failure of pre-packaged, centralized, state provision (Hadley and Hatch, 1981).

The dangers of 'offloading' are, again, implicit in this view; and such scenarios again raise questions about the contemporary reality of 'community' as it is used in such formulations. Even accepting that there may be significant variations in the coherence (Thomas, 1983) and vitality of present-day communities, some would nevertheless still argue that the idea of community is an outdated one – of more use in painting a rather romanticized image of bygone society than providing a basis for informal service provision in the modern world.

Democratization of services

At the other end of the political spectrum advocates of community practice stress the role it can play in contributing to the reconstruction, and thus the strengthening, of public services. Rather than playing a part in curbing, or cutting back, state services, it is seen as a vehicle through which collective provision can be significantly modified, and positively improved. It is here that the justifications for community practice parallel those put forward by democratic-left advocates of decentralization, popular participation in planning, and other reforms aimed at the democratization of public services. The emphasis is put on the importance of restructuring the nature of the transactions between decision-makers and front-line workers, on the one hand, and the user of the service, on the other. It is at this level that people identifying and defining their own needs, as well as taking an active role in implementing programmes to meet those needs, can be encouraged. This is seen as an advance over conventional practice, where, presented with a more or less pre-packaged service, the user is left with only one decision – to take or leave what is on offer.

As we have seen, the orthodox model usually requires that staff draw upon their trained expertise in identifying individual and community needs and interests; it relies upon and reinforces functionally separate forms of provision (while doing little to encourage collaborative inter-agency initiatives); and it tends to render service-users over-dependent on expert personnel, thus restricting and inhibiting users' confidence and ability to take control over significant aspects of their lives. Direct involvement of users and community in the work of service agencies challenges such patterns, leading to a de-mystification and humanization of public-service provision. Doubts and reservations about such a view relate to three issues – its consequences for equity in provision, its consequences for political control and accountability, and its consequences for conventional methods of working by professional experts.

The argument about equity is really the obverse of the argument for flexibility. If a significant part of the case for community practice rests on the need for services to be more adaptable and responsive to community need, then it implies adoption of less rule-bound, less standardized and, in a nutshell, less bureaucratic approaches to provision. However, bureaucracy, as Deakin (1984) reminded us, is one of the most successful devices available for achieving equity, common standards, and fairness in resource allocations. The proper balance between these two sets of desirable objectives and, more importantly, how they are to be reconciled in terms of organizational structures, has yet to be properly addressed in the context of community practice.

Bureaucratic organization makes a further claim – to be the best invention yet to ensure supremacy of politics over administration (Stewart, 1984). In seriously questioning certain aspects of bureaucratic practice, we may also question the supremacy of politics – or, more specifically, the supremacy of centralized, representative-democratic politics as it operates at the local level in Britain.

It may well be feasible to reconcile a significant element of direct democratic participation – a consequence of 'community practice' – with representative democratic decision-making but, again, the exact mechanisms and structures to accomplish this have yet to evolve fully.

A genuine worry is that principled policy formulation at the centre may be undermined by populist action at the front line, an outcome that neither left nor right supporters of community practice could contemplate with equanimity.

Finally, there is the challenge to professional power and interests. Expertise, in both the definition of need and in the organization of services to meet those needs, comes in for increasing scrutiny. The claims for professionalism include specialized expertise, moral veracity, and the service ideal (Wilding, 1982) and these are not to be lightly dismissed. However, professional skills and interests require redefinition if community-orientated forms of practice are to be implemented. For example, technical expertise could be supplemented with enabling and facilitating skills akin to those of the community-development worker.

Conclusion

Clearly, if community practice is to move beyond the purely tokenistic or manipulative, it raises a variety of thorny issues. It poses a threat to the established *modus operandi* of professionals, administrators and politicians, most significantly through the changes it demands in the established structures that support and rationalize the power of those groups. In this sense it poses a significant challenge to conventional ways of doing things, a challenge that goes beyond a modest, reformist tinkering with the organization of service delivery systems.

But to acknowledge this is not to say that the demands of community practice and the interests of those currently committed to more conventional approaches are inevitably or necessarily irreconcilable. Strains and difficulties nearly always attend the introduction of innovations, but there is sufficient evidence to show that community-orientated approaches to service delivery *can* work within existing frameworks of public provision.

So we come back to the central question. If such an approach is *feasible,* are the benefits significant enough to prompt us to extend its implementation – from the experimental and partial to the mainstream and general? We would suggest that it is indeed worthwhile to integrate such an approach into standard practice. It is essential that the main attendant risk – of using it to effect politically motivated 'offloading' – is recognized as a significant issue and explicitly avoided. But, properly implemented, the goals of more responsive, democratic and publicly supported services can, and will, be realized.

References

Adams, R. (1981) *A Measure of Diversion? Case Studies in Intermediate Treatment*. Leicester: National Youth Bureau.

Association of Metropolitan Authorities (1989) *Community Development, the Local Authority Role*. London: AMA

Butcher, H. *et al.* (Eds) (forthcoming) *Community and Public Policy*. London: Pluto Press.

Community Radio Association (1986)

Croft, S. and Beresford, P. (1992) The Politics of Participation. *Critical Social Policy*, Issue 35.

Deakin, N. (1984) *Two Cheers for Decentralisation*, London: Fabian Society.

Donnison, D. (1989) 'Social Policy and the Community', in Bulmer, M. *et al.* (Eds) *The Goals of Social Policy*. London: Unwin Hyman.

Gamble, A. (1988) *The Free Economy and the Strong State*. Basingstoke: Macmillan.

Hadley, R. and Hatch, S. (1981) *Social Welfare and the Failure of the State*. London: Allen and Unwin.

Hadley, R. and McGrath, M. (1984) *When Social Services are Local*. London: Allen and Unwin.

Henderson, P. (1991) *Lessons from a Community Probation Team*. London: Community Development Foundation.

Hoggett, P. and Hambleton, R. (1987) *Decentralisation and Democracy*. Bristol: School of Advanced Urban Studies.

Keane, J. (1988) *Democracy and Civil Society*. London: Vergo.

Mishra, R. (1984) *The Welfare State in Crisis*, Brighton: Wheatsheaf Books.

Plant, R. *et al.* (1980) *Political Philosophy and Social Welfare*. London: Routledge and Kegan Paul.

Stewart, J. (1984) *Decentralisation and Local Government*. London: Fabian Society.

Thomas, D.N. (1983) *The Making of Community Work*, London: Allen and Unwin.

Walker, A. (Ed.) (1982) *Community Care.* Oxford: Basil Blackwell

Wallis, J. and Mee, G. (1983) *Community Schools: Claims and Performance.* University of Nottingham.

Wates, N. and Knevitt, C. (1987) *Community Architecture: How People are Creating Their Own Environment.* Harmondsworth: Penguin.

Wilding, P. (1982) *Professional Power and Social Welfare.* Henley on Thames: Routledge and Kegan Paul.

Willmott, P. (1986) *Social Networks, Informal Care and Public Policy.* London: Policy Studies Institute.

Willmott, P. (1989) *Community Initiatives, Patterns and Prospects.* London: Policy Studies Institute.

Concepts and practice in community leisure and recreation

2

Les Haywood

In the preceding chapter a number of key characteristics of a community-practice approach within public policy were identified, stressing in particular:

- A collective response to needs and problems.
- The importance of co-participation between providers and users.
- Recognition of the value of indigenous resources within community groups.
- Emphasis on the needs of disadvantaged people.
- Recognition of cultural diversity.
- Appreciation of the significance of different dimensions of 'community', e.g. locale, cultural, attachment, interest.

The analysis of concepts and practice in community leisure and recreation in this chapter will examine examples of past and current practice that exhibit some or all of the above characteristics. The extent to which particular cases match the template formed by these criteria is indicative of the variety of approaches that have some claim to legitimately using the term 'community', for it is intended to use the characteristics in an inclusive rather than exclusive manner. However, that is not to say that the title 'community recreation' should be employed lightly, for some examples of current provision simply use the term as a fashionable label, with little or no recognition that a particular set of practices and values is implied. Furthermore, as indicated in Chapter 1, the community approach to public services has been developed as a critical alternative to traditional forms of provision, and therefore it is particularly important to highlight the characteristics that help to define its distinctiveness.

Defining characteristics of community recreation

Focus on 'communities of interest' and disadvantaged groups

An important feature of community recreation is a concern to meet the leisure needs of specific interest groups, especially those that have not benefited from traditional forms of facility provision. Studies conducted from the late 1970s onwards, following the boom in sport-centre construction, which markedly increased the availability of such public facilities, revealed that the majority of users were car-borne, male and middle class. Parallel studies of patterns of participation in the arts and in countryside recreation yielded similar findings in terms of social class. Subsequent concerns over disadvantages emanating from gender, race stereotyping and discrimination, the 'disenfranchisement' of the unemployed, women and ethnic minorities and their consequent under-representation as consumers of publicly provided leisure opportunity, further confirmed these findings.

More recently attention has shifted to the leisure needs of the elderly, as demographic trends increase their significance as consumers (and voters), and to those of handicapped and disabled people, whose rights as full citizens are slowly being recognized. These concerns have led to the widespread identification of such groups as priority targets by many local authorities and by national agencies such as the Sports Council, both in general policy statements and in specific initiatives that have focused attention on particular groupings during particular years, e.g. over-50s, women, youth, etc.

Decentralization of services, localism and devolution of responsibility

The establishment of comprehensive local-authority leisure and recreation departments, corporately managed as parts of the new metropolitan and district councils created in the 1974 reorganization of local government, reflected a then popular belief in the efficacy of large-scale solutions to the provision of public services to large urban populations. By the mid-1980s, however, confidence in these huge and inevitably bureaucratic structures was less marked, and they were under attack from a number of directions. Consumers of services criticized a lack of sensitivity to local needs and alienation from providers. Some elected members felt intimidated by the growing power and specialist professional expertise of the new corporate managers. Financial control and accountability in such large organizations was also questioned, particularly since throughout this period central government grants to local authorities were under stringent review in order to limit public expenditure.

In response to these problems and criticisms some local authorities have adopted more community-orientated approaches to leisure service provision in order to take greater account of locally expressed needs and demands. Decentralization of decision-making has been one solution, usually through the establishment of management committees composed of representatives of users and of the local community in the vicinity of a recreation facility, or handing some control to existing community associations or voluntary organizations. An alternative approach, sometimes related more specifically to the issue of financial control than to community involvement, has been to devolve greater responsibility to facility managers to determine policy locally, offering the potential at least for a greater sensitivity to neighbourhood concerns.

Community development

Community development has been a major rationale for community workers seeking to repair the destruction of traditional working-class communities brought about by urban reconstruction and housing renewal since the Second World War. More recently the creation of new towns such as Milton Keynes and Telford has highlighted the need to develop cohesion and community spirit in order to improve the perceived quality of life among previously disparate populations drawn together for instrumental (economic) reasons. Community development in these contexts has largely been aimed at providing and encouraging local formations within communities that will allow individuals and groups to participate in, or be consulted about, policies affecting their everyday lives.

Leisure and recreation have not featured strongly in such an approach, but where 'community development' is interpreted more widely – literally as the development of a sense of community, or belonging – then it becomes an important medium for growth. Community arts festivals are one such example, for the intrinsically enjoyable events may give rise to the formation of voluntary groups that continue to function after the event, as well as providing a focus for shared fun, celebration and enjoyment. Equally flower festivals provide communities with the common goal of beautifying their environment not simply in order to enjoy its decoration, but to develop a sense of shared effort and local pride extending over much of the year.

Integration with other service provision, e.g. education and training

The use of an integrated approach to the provision of public services has long been promoted as both theoretically efficient in resource and service-delivery terms, as well as offering a more holistic view of people's needs. Corporate management is intended to ensure inter-departmental liaison within local government in order to meet just such goals. However, the reality of corporate management since the establishment of 'modern' local government in the 1970s provides few examples of the integration of leisure and recreation services with other elements of public provision. Education and training, and associated youth and community services, would seem to be an obvious arena for the sharing of resources and for a comprehensive view of young people's needs. Yet there are few cases in which, at a structural level, local government has overtly combined educational and recreational goals.

One exception is Birmingham, which, possibly following critical reviews of its implementation of corporate management in the 1970s, initiated the integration of leisure, education and youth services under the banner of 'Community Education' in the 1980s. Much older examples, dating from the 1940s, are the community colleges established in Cambridgeshire, which were an imaginative attempt to resolve the problems of resource provision and community development in relatively isolated, rural areas. Perhaps the reason for the failure of such experiments to be adopted more widely lies in the narrow and limited conceptions of professional expertise traditionally accepted within local government departments, and the associated jealousy of professional power and influence. A community orientation to service delivery, however, demands decentralization of power, collective approaches to problems and a holistic view of the needs of certain groups, all of which imply a necessity to abandon narrow definitions of the professional roles of teacher, recreation manager, youth worker and so on, and a redefinition of the skills and knowledge of such professionals.

On a small scale it is possible to identify examples of such integrated practice employed by 'task forces' appointed to meet specific needs or solve urgent problems. In Bradford, for example, teachers responsible for providing English language programmes for Asian women have liaised with leisure, health and social service colleagues in order to develop awareness and opportunities across a range of services. In the same metropolitan borough a multi-disciplinary team has sought to use recreational activities for the young unemployed as a medium from and through which to develop education and training in 'life and work skills'. Evidence of a more widespread take-up of such schemes is thin, however, reflecting a mismatch between traditional departmental and professional structures and the use of a holistic approach to social needs and problems – unless motivated by exceptional conditions, such as large-scale immigration and cultural alienation, or threat to social order from disaffected youths.

Methods of delivery of community recreation services

The preceding section has identified four defining characteristics of community leisure and recreation emphasizing both organizational issues, such as decentralization and integration, and those concerned with social goals and values, including the needs of disadvantaged groups and community development and action. We now go on to discuss the variety of methods of actual service delivery associated with a community perspective on leisure and recreation, which, to a greater or lesser degree, exhibit elements of the key characteristics identified with community practice in Chapter 1. In reality of course the methods of delivery and organizational and value issues are implicitly linked, and are inseparable in operation; but for the purposes of analysis they are here treated separately.

'Top down' provider-initiated approaches to resourcing community recreation projects.

This method has been criticized by some proponents of community work as being paternalistic, since it depends on the interpretation of public sector members and officers as to what constitutes a suitable case for action. However, it is difficult for any public policy initiative to avoid this charge, and if it were taken literally, it would be impossible for any such intervention to proceed. But if one ignores this somewhat extreme, purist point of view, it is possible to identify a number of forms of 'top down' provision that meet many of the criteria of community practice.

Direct provision

An example here would be the provision of a community recreation centre deliberately sited in an area of social disadvantage/deprivation and operating a management philosophy consistent with devolution of decision-making to local level, co-participation with clients, recognition of sub-cultural diversity, etc. Examples would include such local initiatives as those described in research in Bradford (Henry, 1984) and more recently in Belfast (Thompson, 1992), and a parallel philosophy underpins the Sports Council's current support for small-scale, local sport halls in preference to larger regional catchment facilities.

Facilitating approach
In this method the public/local authority helps to provide resources to a voluntary or 'mutual aid' group or agency in order to ensure development or continued function. The most common form of facilitation is a monetary grant, and most local authorities make such donations to community groups undertaking various types of charitable work. Grants to leisure and recreation interests are not quite as widespread, although the now defunct Greater London Council saw this as a major means of community development for disadvantaged and special interest groups (Bianchini. 1989). However, Bishop and Hoggett (1986) sound a cautionary note about giving purely financial aid in such circumstances, as it may lead to dependency and undermine the essential character of 'mutual aid' that binds together many recreational groupings.

An alternative form of resourcing is the provision of equipment pools, which are made available to community groups in order to assist with high start-up costs, thus obviating the need for large capital sums. The loan of 'community transport' is another common way in which voluntary groups are supported from public funding, and such transport is frequently vital to the viability of recreational activities. A further form of facilitation is the secondment of local-authority employees in order to provide technical expertise to leisure and recreation groups, one example being sports development officers (often partly funded by the Sports Council or governing bodies of sports). Numerous examples of monetary and resource assistance are assessed in the community recreation experiments described in *Leisure and the Quality of Life* (1977).

Outreach work
This approach, well established in general community work and in youth work, is beginning to be adopted by leisure and recreation providers in order to extend

opportunities to groups that are unaware of, or unable to make use of, mainstream public provision. Outreach workers will have knowledge of local facilities and resources, as well as relevant recreational expertise, and their role is to encourage participation and experimentation in 'new activities'. The concept of 'animation', familiar in continental Europe, in which *animateurs* encourage and provoke community participation in such activities as mural painting, street theatre and sports festivals, provides a well established model of such work. Examples in Britain include the Community Recreation Department in Sheffield, which employs a number of outreach workers whose specific remit is to develop recreational opportunities and experience among selected target groups, including women's organizations, ethnic minorities and the unemployed, in order to combat stereotyping and oppression of such groups (Bramham *et al.*, 1989; see under Bianchini).

Client-led approaches

The majority of leisure and recreation organizations that come nearest to the 'community ideal' of demonstrating a collective approach, cultural diversity, the use of indigenous resources and a sense of place fall into this category. Bishop and Hoggett (1986) characterize these voluntary groups as 'mutual aid', since the rationale for their existence is the need for a collective response in order to render a particular leisure activity viable. Some of these groups are primarily task-orientated, with specific activities and outcomes as their goals, while others are socially orientated, where the socio-emotional rewards of membership are paramount. Many of course provide both such means of potential fulfilment and satisfaction.

Recreation and sports organizations
These are archetypal community leisure organizations, based around the activity interests and enthusiasms of

individuals who draw almost entirely from their own resources in order to provide the necessary expertise, funding and administration. Examples in different spheres of leisure include amateur dramatic and operatic societies, sports clubs, railway preservation societies, and ramblers and conservation associations. Many of these bodies have been characterized as 'middle class' and therefore somehow less legitimately described as 'community'-based. This critique, however, fails to take proper account of the actual membership of these groups, especially sports clubs, many of which are dominated numerically by those in skilled manual occupations (Veal, 1979). It also reveals a limited interpretation of the concept or community.

Community development groups
As discussed above (p.29), the term community development is commonly seen as a process initiated by external agencies through the intervention of community workers. Here, however, we refer to the spontaneous initiation of recreation and leisure projects by members of a community who consolidate its identity and provide a sense of shared purpose even though such aims may not have been overtly stated in advance. Examples would be the formation of a youth sports team by parents concerned at a lack of opportunity for their children, or an allotment-holders' co-operative designed to benefit from the exchange of plants and vegetables and the economies of bulk-buying. The emphasis is heavily on self-help and the identification and use of indigenous resources, and in the process the development of a communal perspective.

Community action groups
Here the emphasis is on the formation of a group in order to bring about change through the adoption and pursuit of a particular cause. Often public authorities are the targets of such action by pressure groups. Local sports councils or playing field associations are

good examples, for although they may have links with larger statutory or voluntary bodies, their essential purpose is to extract resources from a reluctant public sector in order to provide local community facilities, such as an all-weather play area. Somewhat ironically some community action groups are formed in order to curtail the recreational activities of other community organizations, e.g. the campaigns of the League against Cruel Sports against hunting and fishing.

Community service groups
These voluntary groups exist in order to provide a service to other, frequently disadvantaged, members of a local community. There are many cases in the wider fields of personal and social services, such as the British Legion and the Woman's Royal Volunteer Service, targeting respectively ex-service personnel and the housebound. Service groups in leisure and recreation are more limited, but PHAB clubs (physically handicapped and able-bodied) are relatively numerous, and other examples include organizations that provide holidays for mentally handicapped children, such as the Home Farm Trust, or countryside activity breaks for disadvantaged inner city children (the Cinderella Clubs).

Social groups
As indicated above, most client groups are task-centred, but also generate significant social rewards for their members. The reverse of this is the group whose purpose is predominantly social recreation and enjoyment, which may incidently give rise to a wider range of recreational experiences. Working men's clubs (most of which now admit women!) are primarily based on social drinking, together with informal skill and/or chance games such as snooker, bingo, cards and dominoes. However, many clubs promote sports teams, hobby clubs and other interest groups, which extend the level and variety of recreational opportunities on offer. Historically many such clubs began life

as activity clubs, e.g. cycling was a major rationale for their foundation in the period around 1900, before evolving into mainly social entities (Bailey, 1978). Working men's clubs also offer a clear model of a community organization run by and for a largely working-class clientele.

Partnership approaches

Partnerships between voluntary groups and the public sector other than in terms of facilitation, as discussed above, are relatively rare in leisure and recreation. However, as local authorities shift their role from the direct provision of services to one of 'enablement' – a process that has gathered pace under pressure from central government since the late 1980s – it is conceivable that such partnerships will grow. Examples of this approach are schemes in which local authorities buy entertainment or sporting facilities, such as cinemas and football grounds, and then lease them back to community recreation groups, which take on programming and management responsibilities.

An advantage of this sort of co-operation between the public and voluntary sectors is that it permits a degree of experimentation and risk in mounting new community projects that local authorities would be reluctant to pursue alone for fear of incurring long-term financial commitments in areas of uncertain success. Partnerships between the commercial sector and community recreation groups are also a possibility, and are well developed in some activities. Pubs, for example, have long acknowledged the benefits to be derived from the sponsorship of community sports clubs, and more recently have seized on the popularity of quizzes as a means of bolstering trade, actively supporting the development of local leagues and competitions. There are also examples of partnerships between recreational community groups and organized religions as a form of inter-voluntary agency liaison. Historically these associations gave rise to the formation of many football and cricket clubs or choral and operatic societies, which have subsequently become independent organizations (Walvin, 1975).

Management styles and the development of a community recreation approach

Shift from facility to client focus: recognition of community as a resource

A recognition of the shortcomings of traditional forms of public-sector leisure and recreation provision and management in reaching all sections of the community has been partly responsible for the adoption of some of the community recreation approaches discussed in this chapter. In some cases this has led to a thorough reappraisal not simply of management styles *per se,* but of the whole process of identifying community needs, setting aims and objectives, reviewing the status and 'ownership' of facilities and reassessing programming priorities. Table 2.1 illustrates a framework adapted from Williams (1986), which analyses this process as a series of chronologically separable stages that have been developing since the initial establishment of large-scale leisure and recreation departments following local government reorganization in 1974.

Early 1970s – the facility focus
The construction of the first crop of leisure centres reflected a culture in which the facility was central. Technical knowledge and expertise were regarded as the key to managerial success, and concomitant centralized and hierarchical management structures and styles predominated. The attitude to clients was professional in the traditional sense – that of top down dissemination of advice and information within a strict framework of regulation and control defined by

Table 2.1 Towards community recreation provision and management

Dimensions of provision	Facility focus	Activity/group focus	Community focus
Objectives	Maximize income and expertise	Maximize participation	Maximize opportunities
Management styles	Centralized	Decentralized	Decentralized, advocacy, catalytic
Consultation	Professional	Consultant	Partnership
Attitude to clients	Regulation/control of users	Encouragement of under–users	Positive help to the disadvantaged
Perception of facilities	Technical	Service provision/ delivery	Shared resources
Programme emphases	Reactive (e.g.clubs, schools, casual use)	More informal, fun and sociability; elitism played down	Proactive, creative developmental (integrated)
Timescale	Early 1970s	Late 1970s early 1980s	Currently developing

managers. Programming was largely reactive, emphasizing use by existing school and club groups, plus casual uptake of new facilities such as squash courts, for which there seemed to be an insatiable market. Objectives for management centred on the maximizing of use and income and the development of competitive standards of skill and expertise.

Late 1970s, early 1980s – the activity/group focus
Evaluations of the success or failure of the 'facility focus' in reaching all sectors of potential participants coincided with a growing concern for disadvantaged groups that had begun to permeate many sectors of public policy (see, for example, *Recreation and Deprivation*, 1977). This led to a shift of emphasis for managers in which the key objective became the

maximization of participation, which in turn was coupled with a review of the range of activities deployed. In order to achieve these objectives management styles became less centralized, e.g. by shift to area management and/or the appointment of activity leaders, and relations with clients became consultative, focusing heavily on the encouragement of previously under-represented users.

Programming reflected this philosophy, with greater priority going to informal, fun-orientated sessions, stressing sociability and participation rather than competition and elitism. A further consequence of this approach was that the perception of facilities in traditional technical terms began to give way to a perception based on service delivery, so that, for example, swimming pools dispensed with lanes and became leisure pools, and sports areas became multifunctional spaces.

Late 1980s, early 1990s – the community focus
This management approach developed out of the activity/group focus discussed above and in many ways represents an extension of its philosophy rather than a totally different perspective. However, it is radical in the sense that the status of manager–client relations is transformed, with the consequence that the nature of professional roles must undergo significant reappraisal.

In this model management objectives stress the maximization of opportunities for community development and enhancement of the quality of life, with positive discrimination in favour of disadvantaged and deprived groups. Clients are seen as partners with indigenous resources of equal value to the professional knowledge and skills of managers, whose roles change to those of catalyst, advocate and *animateur.* Facilities become shared resources in which 'ownership' lies as much with clients as providers, while programming stresses creativity, responsiveness to change and integration between previously disparate elements of leisure and recreation. A recent example of the latter was the community cultural festival promoted as part of the World Student Games in Sheffield in 1991 (Critcher, 1992).

It cannot be too strongly stressed that these examples of three different management styles, representative of recent trends, constitute 'ideal–typical' models of appoaches employed by various local authorities. It should not be assumed that all leisure and recreation departments have undergone this developmental process towards community recreation – some are still operating with a facility focus, others with an activity/group focus, while yet others may concurrently employ elements of all three approaches. The major use of this framework should be as a means of analysing the current status of public-recreation provision and management by applying it to specific cases at specific times.

Devolution of responsiblities and decentralization within local-authority recreation services

In the previous section the necessity for recreation managers to develop a partnership approach towards clients was identified as a major component in the adoption of a genuine community focus. In parallel with this professional and personal change for managers, community recreation departments have to undergo a complementary reorganisation of management structures and systems in order to realize their aims. The major change necessary is the transformation of hierarchical models, in which policies made at senior political and management levels are handed down via middle managers and thence by supervisors to clients, into more democratic approaches. Such approaches are characterized by two themes: devolution and decentralization.

Devolution of responsibility and decision-making to recreation managers working either in community-based facilities or as outreach workers becomes a necessity if there is to be a genuine commitment to the sharing of facilities, to sensitivity to local needs, and to responsiveness and creativity in dealing with immediate problems. Often an 'immediate' decision is required on allocating funds or resources to a community group if a particular scheme is to succeed and enthusiasm is not to be dissipated by the slowness of response associated with traditional bureaucratic processes. Techniques to allow for such action include (i) allowing local facility managers to decide on specific pricing policies for community groups, reflecting their particular needs and resources; (ii) the establishment of consultative bodies in which members of interest groups such as black people, women, and handicapped and disabled people, meet with local-authority officers from a variety of levels, with delegated power to determine policy and action; (iii) the allocation of funds to a 'community chest' from which small grants may be obtained with a minimum of fuss, provided a necessary degree of accountability is evident and that certain 'community' criteria are met.

Decentralization of management systems implies that not only should leisure and recreation departments physically relocate some of their personnel to the geographical communities they serve and devolve powers from the centre to officers in those locations, but also that their philosophy and methods of consultation should be decentralized. Traditional public service provision relies heavily on the need for elected members (councillors) to consult voters and represent their views in committee decision-making. Frequently such consultation is cursory, if it occurs at all, is subject to 'filtering' by party-political interests and may, or may not, have much impact on the policies jointly determined by senior professional managers and politicians.

By contrast a decentralized concept of consultation should ensure that members of the public have access to local-authority officers at all levels of management within the organization and in all the facilities and initiatives it provides. Equally, politicians should be actively visible at the point of provision in ascertaining and monitoring the views of users/clients and in feeding these views into the policy-making process at appropriate levels. Figures 2.1 and 2.2 illustrate diagrammatically the major differences between a traditional, line management model of recreation policy-making and provision and a community recreation management approach.

It should be noted that the traditional model (Figure 2.1), while essentially a one-way process, does allow some feedback from clients, but such feedback is largely dependent upon the actions of individual users of the service and on the attitudes of specific managers and supervisors. By contrast, the community model (Figure 2.2) is structured so that avenues

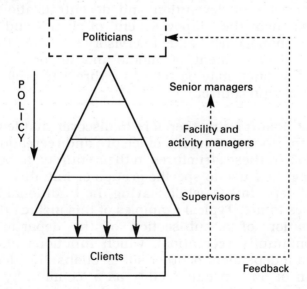

Figure 2.1 Traditional, hierarchical style of recreation management

Figure 2.2 Community, partnership and consultation style of
management

of communication are built into the system to allow
three-way consultation between clients, managers
and politicians in the determination of policies and
practice at all levels of decision-making. These
processes of devolution and decentralization carry
with them the 'empowerment' of clients and lower-
level management and supervisory staff, and the relative 'depowerment' of middle and senior managers,
and as such may be seen as a threat to professional
status and control.

It is unsurprising therefore to discover that few local-
authority departments of leisure and recreation have
adopted these structures in their entirety, at best lim-
iting their use to specific groups or initiatives within
the department, while leaving the traditional hierarchies intact. Typical examples of this include the designation of a sub-section of the department as
'community recreation', which functions alongside
and independent of other sub-sections; the identification of one specific facility as a 'community sports
centre', which operates special policies while other
centres continue in the traditional vein; and the set-

ting up of 'task forces' charged with dealing with particular 'community' problems, such as unemployed youth, ethnic minorities and so on.

The challenge of 'enablement'

In light of the above discussion it is instructive to examine the response of the recreation-management profession to the policies and legislation that Conservative central governments have imposed upon local authorities during the 1980s and early 1990s. The key rationale in these policies is to change the role of local authorities from that of the **direct provider of services,** to one of **enabler of provision.**

Within leisure and recreation this has largely been implemented by the introduction of compulsory competitive tendering (CCT), which requires the 'enabling' local authority to design a contract for the operation of, say, a sports centre, and then invite tenders for the management of that contract for a 5-year period. Bidders for the contract could be the existing public-sector providers themselves, or commercial management operators, and normally the lowest tender must be accepted, provided it meets the desired specifications. The motives of central government ministers promoting these changes are usually seen as political, economic and organizational:

- A *political rationale,* embracing a desire to reduce the powers and scale of local government (especially the mainly Labour-controlled metropolitan boroughs).
- An *economic rationale,* embodying both a pragmatic concern to reduce spiralling costs in local government and their impact on the 'productive' economy, and a philosophical commitment to the primacy of 'markets'.
- An *organizational rationale,* based on the perceived failure of local government to cater efficiently and

responsively to clients' needs, largely as a result of bureaucratic giganticism and professional inertia.

Underlying these motives is a market-liberal philosophy, which identifies the individual consumer's interests as paramount and sets limits on the extent to which government intervention can usefully impinge on people's lives. (Relationships between market liberalism and community are discussed fully in Chapter 3.) Although this philosophy is in some ways at odds with the collective approach identified with community practice, it nevertheless shares a concern with client-centredness and with reducing bureaucratic and professional power. Perhaps it was for these reasons that certain types of community-recreation provision, such as community-centre management, and dual-use education-linked recreation provision, were deliberately excluded from the requirements of CCT. In a sense therefore the policy of 'enablement' presented local government leisure and recreation departments with the opportunity to respond in two broad ways to the legislation:

- To maintain their existing 'managed' provision and submit it to CCT.
- To reorganize provision along community lines, thereby exempting some of it from the tendering process.

In practice the vast majority of departments have taken the former route and have reorganized themselves into 'client' and 'contractor' sections – the former devising the service contract, and the latter bidding under CCT to win the contract and provide the service. In other words, the collective professional stance to the challenge of 'enablement', judging from the published responses of local-authority leisure and recreation departments, and the policies of the Institute of Leisure and Amenity Management (the recreation managers' main professional association), has been conservative, inwardly directed and bureaucratic. Technical and managerial knowledge and skills have been deployed and developed with the primary aim of maintaining control in the hands of existing professionals, and, wherever possible, the provision of services 'in house'. Thus, for example, 'contract writing' and 'tender documentation' have been elevated to the status of high art, with the specification of services pursued in minute detail, ostensibly to protect the service and 'assure quality'. In fact the interests of the public seem frequently to be reduced to bland slogans, while the primary focus of professional activity has been self-preservation.

In sum, the initial professional attitude evoked by requirements of the new legislation has been characterized by recourse to the traditional means by which professions maintain their position, i.e. to use and develop their distinctive professional knowledge (in this case bureaucratic managerialism) both offensively and defensively. Such responses of course expose leisure and recreation managers to the same criticism frequently applied to other established professional groupings, such as lawyers and doctors, which, far from serving the public, in fact become 'a conspiracy against the laity', in the words of George Bernard Shaw. Such critiques revolve largely around the view that professions become obsessed with their own status and self-preservation, manipulate their distinctive professional knowledge in order to extend their exclusivity, misuse their public-service ideal and ethic for their own ends, and in so doing undermine the primacy of their clients' interests as the *raison d'être* for the existence of the profession. Clearly the adoption of 'community recreation' as an alternative response to 'enablement' policies would have entailed both the devolution of powers to community and voluntary organizations and the redefinition of the roles, knowledge and skills of recreation managers, moves that few public-sector recreation professionals seem currently willing to contemplate.

Critical appraisal of the nature of community leisure activities

The foregoing discussion of community recreation in this chapter has been primarily concerned with the processes of provision by seeking to identify the characteristics of a community-practice approach, the methods of service delivery, and the implications for management. Of equal importance in community recreation is the need to examine and reappraise the nature of the leisure activities encouraged and promoted in the name of a public service. This requires a critical and problematizing attitude on the part of providers to such traditional areas as the arts, sports and physical recreation, parks and open spaces, and tourism. Again this may be a difficult exercise for recreation professionals, for it implies the abandonment of cherished values and practices that have been central to their professional education and socialization, and modification of the skills, image and style that have constituted their professional identity. Typical of questions that need to be asked are the following:

- Is leisure simply another area of public provision, like housing or waste disposal, or does its conceptual basis of freedom and choice require a radically different approach to service delivery and management?
- How do traditional art forms relate to community arts, and who are community arts for?
- How may community sports differ from traditional sports? Are some sports better than others for community development?
- How do established city parks serve new city populations? What is a 'community park'?
- How may leisure activities reflect new understanding and thinking on race and gender, age and disability?
- Does tourism aid or injure community development?

● Should public-sector leisure and recreation departments promote 'community and social tourism'?

These fundamental questions focus on the nature
and values of some leisure forms that constitute the
content of community recreation and complement the
processes inherent in a community-practice approach
to public provision. We do not attempt to answer
these questions here as they form the basis to the
chapters in Part Two of this book, in which some
major areas of public provision are examined.

References

Bailey, P. (1978) *Leisure and Class in Victorian
England: rational recreation and the contest for control 1830–1885*. London: Routledge.

Bianchini, F. (1989) 'Cultural Policy and Urban Social
Movements', in Bramham, P. et al. (Eds) *Leisure and
Urban Processes*. London: Routledge.

Bishop, J. and Hoggett, P. (1986) *Organising around
enthusiasms: patterns of mutual aid in leisure.*
London: Comedia.

Critcher, C. (1992) 'Sporting Civic Pride: Sheffield and
the World Student Games', in Sugden, J. and
Knox, C. *Leisure in the 1990s Rolling Back the
Welfare State*. LSA Publication No. 46, Leisure
Studies Association Belfast Conference report.

Haywood, L. and Kew, F. (1989) 'Community
Recreation – Old Wine in New Bottles?, in
Bramham, P. *et al.* (Eds), *op. cit.*

Henry, I.P. (1984) 'Societal Marketing and Leisure
Services'. *Leisure Management*, Jan/Feb. 1984.

Leisure and the quality of life (1977), Volume 2:
Research Papers. London: HMSO.

Recreation and deprivation in inner urban areas
(1977). Department of the Environment, London:
HMSO.

Thompson, S. (1992) 'Three Belfast leisure centres'.
unpublished paper to 1991 LSA conference.

Veal, A. J. (1979) *Sport and recreation in England and*

Wales, Centre for Urban and Regional Studies, University of Birmingham.

Walvin, J. (1975) *'The People's Game': a social history of British Football.* Basingstoke: Macmillan.

Williams, M. (1986) 'Sport and Social Policy', *in Community Provision: the Leicester Experience.* Reading: Institute of Leisure and Amenity Management.

Leisure, market liberalism and community

Maurice Mullard and Norman Borrett

Introduction

In the previous chapters we saw how community recreation evolved to provide a service that met the needs of various client groups, particularly those that were designated 'in need'. Throughout the UK a wide variety of initiatives have been set up within local authorities and through agencies such as the Sports Council and the Central Council of Physical Recreation to identify those who are 'in need' and to provide appropriate facilities and services for them. For example, the Department of the Environment's Recreation Management Training Committee (DoE, 1984) suggested that the manager of recreation services must increasingly assume the role of helper, counsellor and advocate.

The influence of market liberal thinking in the UK and throughout other parts of Europe since the early 1980s has forced providers and managers of recreational services to review the framework within which these goods and services are provided. One major development policy has been the process of 'privatization' of areas of policy that were previously judged as being the responsibility of governments. As governments have sought to respond to the dual pressures of increased demands for public expenditure but also the constraints of taxation, the privatization of certain services has been perceived as being a solution to the problems of financial constraint and also as a possible mechanism for increasing choice for the consumer. The contracting out of recreation services, for example, has placed an emphasis on the more efficient use of resources and better value for money. Since the mid-1980s local authorities in the UK have been compelled by central government to become 'enablers' rather than 'providers' of services.

The major concern of this chapter is to outline an argument showing that it is possible for consumers to be viewed as sovereign in the context of a competitive marketplace, but also that markets do fail and that therefore there can be a role for government intervention within a context that promotes individual choice. Indeed it will be argued that government intervention can promote individual well-being and that the relation between markets and government are compatible. This is particularly evident where public goods are concerned, e.g. parks and open spaces, where the benefit cannot be attributed or 'costed' directly to an individual but contributes to the quality of life for the individual and the community. The concepts of the individual and community are often perceived to be incompatible, since each is related to competing social theory and also ethics. On the one hand, market liberals promote individual self-interest because individuals know best how to pursue their life projects. In contrast, communitarians would argue that the individual is part of a wider community and the community gives the individual rights and privileges – it is the community that makes possible our life projects. While market liberals argue that the individual should be respected as an end and not a means to an end, communitarians emphasize that it is the community and the vision of the 'good society' that should be the end and that individuals represent a means towards the end. At the centre of market liberal theory is the individual, who is described as making rational decisions based on information. In contrast the concept of 'community' is associated with the interests of a collective, which implies either a voluntary response by the community or a positive role for government to promote the interests of the community.

Liberal individualism and the economics of markets

Within a market liberal framework it is always preferable to allow individuals to pursue their self-interest, to make their own decisions as to what goods and services are to be produced in the context of a market economy. The price mechanism is preferred as the best mechanism for the rationing of goods and services. The market guarantees the freedom of choice of consumers to buy services and also the willingness of suppliers to provide services according to a price mechanism signalled through the marketplace. The prices set within the marketplace are perceived to be based on free transactions between individuals. Thus market liberals would emphasize that it is the individual who is best placed to define what constitutes leisure. Since the individual is perceived to be rational, there can be no ordering as to what preferences are to be prioritized. The individual is treated as an end rather than a means to an end. Each individual carries a different vision of the good society, and is to be given equal status without anyone having the right to impose his/her vision on others.

Market liberalism and the individual

Market liberals take as given the argument that individuals left to themselves would always choose to live within the context of the marketplace. However, market liberals are also aware that individuals may combine in order to subvert the climate of competition and thus act against the interest of individual consumers. Market liberal theorists accept therefore that there is a need for government to regulate the tendency towards mergers and monopolies that might act against the public interest. According to Hayek, Friedman and Brittan (Green, 1987), there is a role for government to promote the climate of market liberalism. In this sense government policy has to be conducted in such a way that benefits the individual and not specific interest groups

Market liberalism advocates that government policy should be conducted through a process of law and procedures that ensure equality of treatment of all individuals. Individual liberty can only be guaranteed if government conducts itself in the context of rules, including a written constitution that ensures the separation of powers within government, and that majorities do not vote in such a way as to erode or put into question individual rights. According to market liberals, public policy should be guided through a series of rules and principles that are publicized so that the individual is made aware of the conduct of government. Hayek says 'the great aim of the struggle for liberty has been equality before the law. This equality under the rules which the state enforces may be supplanted by a similar equality of the rules that men voluntarily obey in their relations with one another' (1984), p. 80).

The concepts of rational agent and rational choice

Individuals are defined as rational agents because they know best, and since they know best, no one else has the right to announce on behalf of the individual what real need is, or to put order on preferences or to moralize on behalf of the individual, The role of government should be to provide the context which is based on rules that protect the right of self-interest. Government does not encourage a selfish morality by legitimizing self-interest but rather 'enables' a process that ensures the freedom of the individual against the more arbitrary morality of others.

The individual is described as rational because (1) she/he has natural competence and (2) has technical competence. Natural competence denotes the ability to maximize individual well-being. Technical competence means the ability to be strategic in making choices, since alternatives carry costs. Natural and technical competencies represent the process of evaluating the costs and benefits in making accurate choices, searching for information and making decisions based on that information. Decisions individuals make are founded on information they have available. Such decisions could be different, if different information were available. Only the market is sufficiently flexible to respond to changes in decisions, which themselves depend on the state of knowledge at a certain point.

The individual and the market

Markets are not fixed; the type and number of goods provided represent the revealed preferences at a specific place and at a specific time. Definitions of what constitutes leisure and the costs of leisure are also continuously revealed through the spontaneity of the market as opposed to centralized planning. It is, according to Hayek, the spontaneous decisions of individuals that change the nature of the marketplace. Individuals as suppliers are willing to provide leisure facilities because they have a view about other individuals who want to buy the services they provide. A marketplace where there are buyers and sellers therefore exists. The competitive marketplace is described as being the context guaranteeing consumer sovereignty. It is because there are a large number of buyers and sellers with no barriers to entry that markets are non-discriminatory. The marketplace is best described as a process where buyers and sellers meet and make prices. The price set represents the willingness to buy by the consumer and also the willingness to sell by the supplier, a price that is of mutual benefit.

The dynamics of supply and demand

The theory of markets suggests that suppliers and buyers of goods and services meet in the marketplace. The price mechanism allows for all goods to be cleared at a certain price. If suppliers signal a price that is too high, then supply will outstrip demand, goods will be left on the shelves unsold, signalling to the supplier a wrong price. Suppliers now have the choice to reduce the price to clear their shelves – the price mechanism therefore becomes the signal to buyers and sellers.

The consumer is described as sovereign in the context of market competition. Competitive markets reflect the preferences of consumers and these revealed preferences are reinforced by the price mechanism, the willingness to buy goods and also the willingness of suppliers to produce them. Consumer sovereignty means that the individual is the price-maker, because under competitive markets consumers can choose between competitive prices. In this context the consumer influences the goods supplied and the price.

Since rationality represents decisions based on current knowledge, then market economists would argue that as knowledge and information changes so will the decisions made by the rational individual. The Pearce Report (1989), *A Blueprint for a Green Economy*, utilizes the concepts of supply and demand and prices to provide the necessary solutions to the problems of the environment. Pearce argues that as the individual becomes more knowledgeable about environmental costs, the environment will not be assumed to be a 'free' resource, and that like all other goods the environment carries a positive value and therefore a price. The pollution of a river by a firm might be seen as no cost to the firm but it is a cost to the community. Pearce suggests that governments should impose a tax on the environment or make the polluter pay. This will in turn increase the price of goods reflecting the environmental costs, and

> ...the elementary theory of supply and demand tells us that if something is provided at a zero price more of it will be demanded. For example by treating the ozone layer as a resource with a zero price there was never an incentive to protect it... The important principle is that resources and environments serve economic functions and have positive economic values... This simple logic underlines the importance of valuing the environment correctly and integrating these correct values into economic policy (Pearce *et al.*, 1989, p. 5 and 7).

According to Pearce, governments should now put a cost on the environment as part of economic policy. A policy of economic growth has to be costed in relation to the impact on the environment so that unlimited growth in future will not necessarily be taken to be a desirable objective. Instead a 'sustainable' growth policy, one that takes into account the costs on the environment, will be preferred. Equally, governments in future will have to make decisions on transport policy by deciding on the costs and benefits of providing subsidies for public transport as against the environmental costs of expanding private transport. On all these issues the environment enters the equation as a price for both the consumers and suppliers.

The concept of market failure

While all market economists would argue that the market economy is the most effective means of resolving the twin problems of economic efficiency and equity, they also recognize that the price mechanism may not deal with all questions of importance to the individual. The recognition that markets might not address some issues is usually treated within the framework of 'market failure'. Friedman and Friedman (1980) would argue, for example, that there are cases in which state intervention can be legitimated within the framework of market liberal principles. These include:

1 As a neutral arbitrator between conflicting and competing interest groups (an example would be the tensions between countryside conservation and tourism development in rural areas).
2 To overcome imperfections in the operation of the free market such as the impact of monopolies on local communities, and the notion of 'neighbourhood effects'. In the latter case non-users or free riders benefit from the investment of others, e.g. in the provision of services where it is uneconomic to collect fees (parks and open spaces, coastal areas, etc.).
3 A paternalistic approach for support in very special circumstances, e.g. provision for people with disabilities.

The next section outlines three major areas of market failure that legitimize a role for government in a way that actually enlarges the freedom of the individual. Brittan (1988) calls this agenda for government a moral political economy, since it provides guidelines for intervention aimed at benefiting the individual as against benefiting vested interest groups.

Market failure – the problem of externality

The problem of externality implies that the social costs are not properly internalized by the individual pursuing self-interest. The concept of externalities in the context of market economies confirms that there might be conflicts between individuals and the interests of the wider community. Externalities provide an agenda for intervention by government. The concern with pollution and the environment, and decisions to invest in education can be categorized as examples of the problems of externalities.

The environment

One major externality problem in contemporary society is concerned with the issue of pollution and the protection of the environment. The concern for market liberals is how to provide a policy that protects the environment but also individual liberty. Market liberals would argue that the problem of environmental damage is related to price, and that in previous generations it was assumed that the environment was a free commodity and could therefore be used at a nil cost. As already suggested earlier, the Pearce Report (1989) has advocated using the price mechanism and the policy of the 'polluter pays' to control pollution. Market liberals would therefore argue that governments should use the tax system to alter consumer behaviour, to put a price on environmental costs and thereby reduce pollution. The tax changes on petrol and increases in VAT on domestic fuels can be seen as policies seeking to influence consumer behaviour.

Education policy as human capital investment

A second area of discord between individual self-interest and social cost arises in the context of education and training. The concept of self-interest addresses issues of education as a form of investment in the person; that is when education becomes a decision of investment in human capital. However, the provision of education is too complex to be left to individual decisions, since most individuals do not have sufficient information or resources to invest accurately in their futures. If education decisions are left to individuals, then there will be an under-investment in education by many sections of the population, with consequent harmful effects on the economy and the community. Within this context it is necessary for governments to intervene in the provision of education services, and most market liberals recognize education and training as a legitimate case of externality.

Market failure – public goods theory

The concept of a public good suggests that there are certain public goods that do not easily transfer into commodities and prices. The nature of these goods suggests that it is society at large that benefits and that costs and advantage cannot be attributed to an individual. Examples of public goods would include the public provision of parks, gardens and public libraries. Society at large benefits from a good quality public library. A library is there to provide information; thereby the cost of information is now shared by the community yet individuals become better informed. It is society that benefits from decisions which are made in the context of a better informed public.

Parks and gardens represent places of public access which, if left to individual self-interest to provide and enjoy for a price, would no longer be considered as spaces of public access but private properties. Since it is central to market liberals that individuals do not live like atoms but are individuals in the context of a society that respects the rights of the individual, areas of public access confirm the relation between the society and freedom of the individual. Again, public places represent public goods because the benefits derived by the individual and society cannot be transferred into costs upon identifiable individuals.

Market failure – income distribution

Market liberal theorists vary in their views on the extent to which governments should intervene in the economy in order to deal with differences in income between individuals in society. At one extreme writers such as Hayek (1988) argue that differences in income are the natural outcome of individual freedom, that ownership of property confirms the right of the individual to define self-interest, and that attempts by government to redistribute income and wealth are against the interests of individuals, and dysfunctional to society. Hayek therefore argues against such discriminatory practices as progressive income taxes, arguing for a flat rate irrespective of income, and taxes on consumption and spending rather than on incomes.

On the other hand, market liberals such as Rawls (1988) and Brittan (1988) have suggested that it is possible that the rights of the individual can be preserved in a context where questions of redistribution are also addressed. Rawls argues that in order to operate efficiently societies need to ensure that individuals have equal opportunities and access to positions and careers. If lack of wealth prevents them from fully exploiting their abilities, then there exists a legitimate rationale for state intervention in order to make best use of resources. A further argument suggests that income inequality is legitimate only if it can be shown to benefit society as a whole, e.g. because clear income differentials provide incentives for high earners to generate economic activity, which in turn creates opportunity for widespread prosperity for individuals of varying abilities. However, if individuals do not believe that such a process genuinely benefits those on low incomes, and that the resulting inequalities are unfair and are likely to carry social costs, then they may decide that income redistribution is more likely to be in their own, and others' rational self-interests. As Rawls suggests, individuals may thus decide within a framework of market liberalism to replace the 'difference principle' by the 'democratic principle', which implies a more egalitarian stance.

In the following discussion of market liberalism and community recreation these issues of inequality of opportunity and access, and of attempts to compensate for wealth differences by such policies as targeting disadvantaged individuals, will be discussed within the concept of 'market failure'.

Market liberalism and community leisure

Within the context of leisure policy certain issues can be located as examples of market failure. According to market liberal arguments, the present erosion of footpaths can be attributed to the absence of markets and the inability of the Countryside Commission adequately to identify suppliers and consumers. Equally, market liberals have sought to intervene in the debate on the recent sales of works of art and asked whether Hans Holbein's 'Portrait of a Lady' and Constable's 'The Lark' could be perceived as part of the National Heritage and treated as 'public goods' rather than as marketed commodities. Furthermore, although there are many leisure activities provided within the marketplace, it might be argued that certain forms of leisure do represent pure public goods, since no individual consumer and supplier can be identified and also that the public goods seek to promote the well-being of the community. One such example of a public good is countryside recreation and activities such as walking and sightseeing, where the scenery and the environment can be perceived to be free goods to be enjoyed by the community. The problem for the market economist is how to allocate the costs of erosion and how to protect the countryside for future generations. Market economists would seek to argue that governments need to set a price on the costs to environment, and use the price mechanism as the means of rationing and preserving footpaths.

We shall now consider three case-study examples that locate the principles of market liberalism within community leisure. The case studies have been chosen to illustrate different aspects of leisure provision and how a market liberal analysis serves to explain elements of access, provision, choice and control.

Case study 1 The countryside – a case of public goods

> During the post-war era, opportunities for the people of Britain to roam the countryside have steadily been reduced... As those who own land have devoted ever more of it to the ever more intensive pursuit of wealth, they have eliminated much of the hitherto marginal areas... that made walking both possible and enjoyable (Marion Shoard, 1987, p. 537).

Market forces in the countryside

In Marion Shoard's lucid and powerful portrayal of the struggle over Britain's countryside, *This Land is Our Land,* the increasing privatization and exploitation of our rural environment is explored. Left to market forces, our countryside would be at the mercy of powerful landowners, developers and entrepreneurs. The great majority of the countryside is privately owned and current evidence suggests that ownership is becoming more concentrated in the hands of fewer people.

Another issue of concern is the devastation of our countryside through modern farming methods. The 6 years from 1978 to 1984, for example, witnessed the destruction of 17,500 miles of hedgerow, the construction of over 100,00 new farm buildings, and the clearance of nearly 100 square miles of deciduous woodland. Furthermore, plough damage to archaeological sites has resulted in many burrows, forts and bronze age settlements being destroyed (Shoard, 1987).

The changes that have taken place in the countryside over the past 25 years have resulted in restricted access to the remaining sites of peace and beauty. Many of our public rights of way in England and Wales are obstructed with impunity. For example, a research study at Reading University in 1984 found that in the nine parishes that comprised the study area, 59 per cent were not restored. Another example of market forces at work is the tens of thousands of acres of woodland sold by the Forestry Commission to the private sector during the 1980s. As access was originally only on a 'permissive' basis, the new private landowners were free to terminate access and enclose the woodlands for their own amusement or development (Shoard, p. 342–3).

There are many other examples of enclosure, destruction, privatization, and exploitation in Shoard's disturbing analysis, but the above examples demonstrate the dangers of a free-market approach to countryside management and policy-making. For these, and other reasons, many of the features of our rural environment – woodlands, footpaths, bridleways, streams, hedges, and open spaces, are treated as public goods. This legitimates government intervention in the market to protect such amenities for society and future generations.

Since it is the process of market economics that has been largely responsible for damaging our countryside, radical solutions are needed. One such solution could be taxation to regulate economic activity in order to protect public goods. According to Shoard, one form of taxation could be a rural land tax to be paid annually on each acre of rural land. This would serve to counteract the financial incentives associated with landscape destruction. To be effective, the tax would need to be levied negatively as well as positively, so an element of redistribution would take place.

As an example, a Yorkshire farmer who owns lowland heath containing the increasingly rare and beautiful ultramarine marsh gentian may decide to preserve the land rather than draining it for commercial development and hence gain a land tax subsidy. There is of course considerable state intervention already in rural economics but the policy tends to be fragmented and haphazard (examples include inheritance tax exemption and farm capital grants). Because the land tax involves the redistribution of wealth within the landowning community, there would be no additional cost to the Exchequer.

Public goods and public footpaths

A market-driven approach assumes that economic goods can be priced in the market. This is fine as long as the benefit of such goods or services can be confined to those who pay. Clearly, there are many goods and services that cannot be priced in this way, since anybody can benefit as a 'free rider' (enjoyment by an extra person because this does not impose a sacrifice on others).

While it is possible to estimate the value of rights of way to the farmer or the local authority in terms of opportunity gain, it is not easy to calculate the benefits to users or the costs in losing the amenity. Estimating the value of recreational walking or bird-watching to the user will need an analysis of psychological and perhaps physiological benefits, resulting in spillover gain that is difficult to quantify.

Thus public goods must be paid for collectively and financed through, say, subscription, sponsorship, or taxation. In the case of public rights of way the government intervenes in the market through legislation (especially planning control), and by taxation collects monies for the upkeep and development of these amenities.

Case study 2 Broadcasting – public goods versus consumer choice

The television set and the radio form the centrepieces of home-based broadcasting entertainment. Nearly 60 per cent of households have two TV sets, with around 17 per cent having three sets. Radio listening is increasing, with around 70 million radio sets in the UK; the average household possesses four sets and 20 per cent of households claim to have six sets or more!

The Conservative governments of the 1980s embarked on a policy of increased competition and efficiency in both TV and the radio industries. However, within the framework of greater competition the BBC and IBA have been required to fulfil certain programming obligations that were set out in government regulations (at least, until 1988). Within these regulations exists the fundamental principle of public-sector broadcasting, which required programmes of high quality for the public good. 'Public sector broadcasting is understood to imply an obligation to inform and educate as well as entertain, and to reflect a proper balance and a wide range of subject matter' (Bennett, 1991, p. 41).

This notion of a public good represents an attempt by government to 'regulate' the market, ensuring a balance of programmes that reflect diversity and plurality of interests. In contrast to the BBC and ITV companies, cable and satellite companies have few (if any) regulations governing quality or balance.

In 1988 the government published a then White Paper on the future of broadcasting, indicating its intention to give market forces greater emphasis. This White Paper culminated in the new Broadcasting Bill (1989). At the heart of the new bill is the consumer who is allowed greater choice by exercising his/her preference within a free market. Hence there are new satellite and cable TV companies and more local and regional independent radio companies in competition with one another in the market.

A major concern in allowing greater market influence is whether high standards (however defined) might be eroded. The government has, to a limited degree, protected standards by incorporating 'quality' principles within the process of tendering for contracts. However, the new 'lighter touch' regulations mean that the obligation on all independent broadcasting companies to provide a full range of programmes has been removed.

The government as regulator

We live in a society in which the government often acts as a regulator (through the legislative system) to control market forces. This takes place with the general approval of the community, who vote for a curtailment of individual freedom in order to enhance the interests of the community.

Consumers are protected, in a number of ways, from elements of market failure, as follows:

1 The state regulates to protect consumers from programmes that might offend against taste, decency or public feeling, or programmes that might encourage crime or disorder.
2 The presentation of news needs to be accurate and impartial.
3 Those who provide the service should omit bias regarding religious, political or public policy matters.
4 Advertising should be subject to the same requirements as 1–3 above (Bennett 1991, p. 42–3).

Under the franchise licences it will be up to the broadcasting companies what to show and when to show it. It is the viewer that will now be responsible for quality and diversity of programmes. However, the new process of competitive tendering for each franchise has meant that companies have submitted inflated bids to secure a franchise and this limits the funds available to produce quality, i.e. more expensive programmes. Critics of the competitive franchising, system suggest that the careful development of a responsible and highly regarded broadcasting system is now threatened by indiscriminate free-market interests.

We saw earlier that at the heart of market liberalism is the individual who makes decisions based on information. Thus individuals know best what they want to consume and would see government interference in broadcasting as an infringement on liberty and ultimately distorting the efficiency of the market. Because the individual is perceived as being rational, there should be no ordering or prioritizing of preferences by any outside agency.

In contrast to such 'pure' market liberals, others recognize that there are circumstances when 'costs' and 'benefits' have to be balanced. Hence it is legitimate to legislate (at the cost of individual freedom) to protect the greatest happiness of the greatest number. It is therefore appropriate for the government to intervene through the legislative system to promote the general welfare of all. However, there is a fine dividing line between individual freedom (to watch pornography, for example) and regulation (who are the moral gatekeepers?).

Supply and demand in broadcasting

We have seen that in a free market suppliers and consumers come together to agree a price. In the case of broadcasting the public will 'purchase' programmes through subscription or licence or by buying the appropriate satellite or cable hardware. The individual is the price-maker in a free market because the consumer can choose between competitive suppliers. Hence the consumer can influence the quality and quantity of programmes through the process of demand and supply.

Market failure

The concept of market failure assumes a 'moral' political economy that protects the interests of the individual in special circumstances. In the case of broadcasting a free market may allow the import of cheap, foreign programmes that in the short term satisfy the demand of consumers. However, this policy may lead to the decline and eventual termination of 'quality' programme-makers in the UK. This may not be in the long-term interests of consumers, as choice may ultimately be limited.

This also raises the question of 'public goods' and whether certain programmes need to be protected as part of our national heritage. Within the arts, public goods might be companies such as the Royal Opera House, the Royal Ballet, and the Royal Philharmonic, which transmit their productions to a wider audience via radio and television. These are considered 'minority' areas of consumption and may suffer terminal decline if left to free market forces.

Bennett (1991) argues that programme diversity and increased choice are essential to the concept of consumer sovereignty, and questions whether greater market forces will produce increased diversity. Advertising, for example, requires a high viewer profile, and the independent sector is very much dependent on advertising revenue; thus the incentive is to present those programmes which will attract high numbers of viewers. Bennett recognizes a tension between an increasingly competitive broadcasting environment and a commitment to programme diversity and quality.

Case study 3 Community leisure – income redistribution and externalities

This case study is concerned with the issue of income redistribution and the responses of market liberals to problems of access to leisure opportunities where income is a major barrier to entry. Since the emphasis of market liberalism is the individual, the absence of opportunities for individuals to explore their life projects and personal capacities are judged as resulting in inefficiency and ineffectiveness. Market liberals would recognize that leaving the market to itself would lead to income inequalities, with only those on high incomes being able to pursue their life projects. In the context of income distribution, market liberals would recognize a problem of market failure and would argue for government to intervene in the process of income redistribution.

This position has, for example, been outlined by the Institute of Economic Affairs (Green, 1987) in its approach to vouchers for education and health care. Market liberals, in constructing an argument for income distribution, see a role for government as an 'enabler' rather than as a 'provider' of a service. In making a commitment to income distribution the state does not have to be the provider of a service but is conceived as a vehicle that facilitates individuals getting the resources that then give those individuals the freedom of choice to purchase the service.

Within the context of leisure policy the concept of community recreation can be perceived as a response to issues of income distribution and the externalities (in terms of social costs) arising from such inequalities. The term 'community' has many meanings. Early views of community life were rooted in the concept of a 'moral community' and this was seen to contain the following elements:

- A sense of identification and belonging.
- Moral unity and a sense of following common goals.
- Involvement and participation in groups.
- Wholeness, in which individuals regarded each other as having intrinsic worth (Murphy and Howard, 1977).

In the context of modern society many of the aspects outlined above have been eroded. Today some communitied exhibit elements of 'anomie' and moral fragmentation (Murphy and Howard, 1977 p. 60). Members of some modern communities are perceived to be self-interested and concerned with their own fulfilment to the detriment of others. This ultimately leads to tension and finally a fracture in the very foundations of a civil society.

We have seen earlier that communitarians seek government intervention in the market as necessary to protect the interests of community. This would result in support for those redistributional policies leading to equality of opportunity (Rawls, 1988). The issue of equality of opportunity is central to the notion of community recreation because one of the key concerns of community recreation is to devise policies that meet the needs of disadvantaged groups. For example, government has directly intervened in the market process by allocating funds for new and improved sports provision following civil unrest (inner-city riots).

These funds have been allocated on the basis that they will meet the needs of specific target groups, e.g. young unemployed Afro-Caribbeans in Brixton, and assist in overcoming civil disorder by channelling energies into socially approved leisure activities, i.e.

wholesome recreation. Clearly the market (commercial providers of recreational goods and services) will not supply recreational goods unless there is seen to be an appropriate return on investment, i.e. a return for shareholders and profit for reinvestment. Owing to market failure, intervention can be legitimated within the framework of a 'moral political economy' (Brittan, 1988). Hence, within a utilitarian perspective emerges a pragmatic approach to individualism that balances costs and benefits to society, resulting in the happiness of the greatest number, that is the streets are safe from civil unrest and individuals can once more pursue self-interest.

The sovereign rights of individuals

We demonstrated earlier how, within one market liberal perspective, the imposition of progressive taxation should be avoided (Hayek, 1988). Similarly, any process of positive discrimination in leisure provision such as 'passports' or vouchers for groups 'in need' would contravene the sovereignty of the market. The rights of the individual must always come before any claims of the 'general good' and any element of redistribution (whether through means-tested vouchers, or other forms of redistribution) must be avoided. The problem with such a stance, however is that the freedom of the individual to pursue self-interest can be constrained by the elements of market failure referred to earlier. Hence interference in the market of recreational provision may be justified if the process results in enhancing individual liberty generally.

Equality of opportunity and access

It has also been demonstrated that contractual market liberalists such as Rawls (1988) support a notion of justice in which the rights of individuals can be protected *and* questions concerning the redistribution of resources addressed. Rawls' notion of 'just entitlement' supports equality of opportunity and access partly because income inequality denies certain individuals the right of self-interest. Thus, in the context of recreational opportunity and choice, a policy of 'community recreation' would support the notion of 'just entitlement' and at the same time protect the rights of the individual. To see how this is achieved it is necessary to examine the characteristics of community recreation.

Community recreation has developed partly to overcome the limitations and shortcomings of facility-led approaches to recreation management based on income maximization. As indicated in Chapter 2, four key issues are addressed in community recreation:

1 *Positive discrimination* – meeting the needs of particular interest groups and targeting those groups levelled as 'disadvantaged'. It was recognized in the early stages of recreation management that income inequality acts as a barrier to entry and opportunity, hence the right of 'self-interest' for some individuals is denied. This may lead to 'anomie' within the social system, and so intervention in the market is legitimated because the interests of the community can enhance individual liberty.
2 *Decentralization of services* – smaller-scale, neighbourhood, administrative centres can deal best with the needs of diverse community groups. Local organizations are sensitive to the needs of community groups and are more visibly accountable. Through the establishment of local cost-centres resources can be redistributed to maximize the expectations of the least advantaged under conditions of fair equality of opportunity (Rawls, 1988).
3 *Community development* – the effectiveness of decentralization depends upon those mechanisms and structures within communities that allow consultation, participation, action and ultimately the maximization of self-interest. Community groups

need to take part in the planning and policy-making process so that they can see justice is done through the equitable distribution and redistribution of goods. Thus intervention in the free market to enhance community development is justified because individual self-interest is being met more efficiently (by contrast, the social costs incurred by non-intervention would reduce freedom for the individual).

4 *Integration of services* – community recreation does not happen in isolation from other personal social services such as education, health care, or employment. Indeed, the 'needs' of individuals are often complex and require a multi-service approach, which demands efficient service integration. Community recreationalists operating on the basis of 'care' and equity do not limit their endeavours to recreation *per se* but are concerned about 'wholeness', i.e. the complete well-being of the individual. As an example, a community recreation outreach worker acting as an *animateur* in a depressed inner-city environment establishes contact with a group of young mothers. Some of these mothers are in need of health care as a result of drug abuse, heavy smoking and alcoholism, others require re-housing, and others are in need of advice on social welfare and employment opportunities. By understanding the social problems in the community the community recreation worker can respond with advice and action that can begin to address some of the problems of market failure. Dealing with these problems of externality may well increase the opportunities for self-interest for others.

The four elements of community recreation result in setting particular and distinct management and economic objectives. Table 3.1 is adapted from Chapter 2 and contrasts elements of community-recreation practice with that of market liberalism.

Community recreation and market liberal approaches to recreation provision

In Chapter 2 Haywood discusses a shift in management thinking from a focus on facilities and provision in the early 1970s to an emphasis on activities and target groups in the late 1970s and early 1980s, and then to a community focus from the mid-1980s onwards. The community recreation approach has been concerned with how policy is decided and the intention for such policies, i.e. an evaluation of what the policies are expected to achieve. Thus there has been a philosophy based on the maximization of opportunity, particularly for those 'in need'. Clearly any financial objectives under the community-recreation umbrella will have to allow for the provision of services that are affordable to those in need, and this usually means subsidized provision for designated target groups.

Table 3.1 Community-recreation and market liberal approaches to recreation provision

Dimensions of provision	Community recreation focus	Market liberal approach
Philosophy	Enrichment of life by collective action	Framework for markets and individual choice
Financial objectives	To provide a service that is affordable by all, but particularly those in need	Low costs, productivity, profits
Management styles	Decentralization, advocacy, catalytic, use of volunteers	Professionals, experts to ensure efficiency and maximum returns
Programme emphasis	Proactive, creative, developmental, equitable	Consumer–orientated approach
Attitude to clients	Caring, positive help to those in need	Customer care

We can see from Table 3.1 that market liberalism is based on the provision of a framework for markets with the key financial objectives of productivity, value for money, and profit (or loss limitation). The management style, the programme emphasis, and the attitude to clients changes from a focus on equity and a concern to identify 'those in need', to a service that concentrates on the efficiency of resource allocation and take-up. Thus, in market liberalism, there is a concern to improve the quality of management, the maximization of use of resources, and greater efficiency in service delivery. This process will, it is argued, improve access and opportunity for all.

Despite differences in focus, there are areas of compatibility between community recreation and market liberal approaches. For example, both approaches are concerned with the effects of market failure and we have seen earlier (Friedman and Friedman, 1980) that there are occasions when intervention can be legitimated, e.g. paternalistic approaches to support people with disabilities, a concern for externalities and income distribution, and the notion of public goods.

Conclusions

The major concern of this chapter has been to outline the core principles that can be described as constituting a market liberal perspective and the implications of this approach for leisure policy-making. It was suggested that within the framework of 'market failure' market liberals are able to produce an agenda for government intervention that can still adhere to the ethics of liberalism. Market liberals would argue that the attempt to construct such an agenda for government would mean that government intervention would be founded on moral principles as against political judgement, political calculation and political expediency.

At the centre of the market liberal perspective is the individual, who is perceived as being capable of making rational choices and whose decisions are of equal value to decisions made by other individuals. Within this context individuals have to be seen as ends being responsible for life projects rather than as means to an end, where it is the vision and life projects of society or the community that are more central. According to the market liberal, it is individuals who decide what constitutes the good society rather than for governments to impose the vision of the good society. Since individuals are continuously engaged in decision-making, the marketplace is the mechanism that allows for individuals to reveal their choices and priorities. Within the marketplace all individuals are treated as rational consumers, which makes the market more just than the political process, which by contrast is perceived to be arbitrary and often serving the vested interests of functional groups rather than individuals.

The concept of public goods implies that there are certain areas of human activity that are not readily transferable into marketed commodities. Libraries and parks provide opportunities that cannot be targeted at individuals. The access to public libraries and the opportunity for a society to become better informed cannot be costed on individual users, since the aim of libraries is to encourage access. Within the context of historic buildings and works of art the concept of national heritage for example suggests that the costs of allowing a major work of art to be sold and exported would be a major loss and that governments should intervene for the benefit of future generations.

In contrast, in areas where markets for leisure are clearly discernible, a role for government only as regulator can be justified within the context of market liberalism. The UK government policy on broadcasting confirms that the distribution of information cannot be left entirely to the market, hence a role for public service broadcasting in this area. However, the majority of broadcasting is open to market forces.

The problem of income distribution is also of concern to market liberals, since income may be the determining factor in deciding the opportunities available to individuals. Thus, within the context of income inequality, individuals on low incomes would not be able to explore their capacities, which means that the economy as a whole would not be operating at an efficient level. Markets liberals therefore advocate that government should seek to influence the distribution of income either through a policy of negative income tax or providing vouchers to those on low incomes to purchase services. Within the context of income distribution the government acts as an enabler, providing individuals with the means to consumer services rather than becoming a provider of services.

Community recreation provision, targeted on specific groups, is a key example of the recognition of the problem of income distribution, and is thus regarded by market liberals as a legitimate arena for intervention by local government. Community-recreation approaches are thus compatible with the economic criteria of liberals (using the concept of market failure) and also resonate well with some of the philosophies about the freedom of the individual, since community practice emphasizes the importance of individuals in determining their own leisure needs, and the formation of voluntary mutual aid groupings. However, at the same time those aspects of community practice that celebrate 'collective action' as a positive value – as a vision of the good life in which individuals are only a means – rest less easily with the principles of market liberals.

References

Ackerman, B. (1980) *Social Justice in the Liberal State.* Yale University Press.

Bennett, O. (1991) 'Entertainment and the Arts', in Borrett, N. (Ed.). *Leisure* Services UK, Macmillan.

Brittan, S. (1988) *A Restatement of Economic Liberalism.* 2nd edition, Macmillan.

Clarke, J. and Critcher, C. (1985) *The Devil Makes Work: Leisure in Capitalist Britain.* Macmillan.

Friedman, M. and Friedman, R. (1980) *Free to Choose.* Harmondsworth: Penguin.

Gray, J. (1989) *Liberalisms: Essays in Political Philosophy.* London: Routledge.

Green, D. (1987) *The New Right.* Brighton: Wheatsheaf.

Harvey, J. (1987) Urban Land Economics, 2nd edition. Macmillan Education.

Hayek, F.A. (1984) 'Value and Merit', in Sandel, M. (Ed.) *Liberalism and its Critics.* Oxford: Basil Blackwell.

Hayek, F.A. (1988) *The Fatal Conceit, The Errors of Socialism.* London: Routledge.

Haywood, L. and Henry, I. (1986) 'Policy Developments in Community Leisure and Recreation', *Leisure Management,* Vol. 6, Nos 7 and 8.

Kymlicka, W. (1990) *Contemporary Political Philosophy: An Introduction.* Clarendon Press.

Mulhall, S. and Swift, A. (1982) *Liberalism and Communitarians.* Basil Blackwell.

Murphy, J.F. and Howard, D.R. (1977) *Delivery of Community Leisure Services: An Holistic Approach.* USA: Lea and Febiger.

Nozick, R. (1974) *Anarchy, State and Utopia.* Basil Blackwell.

Pearce, D. Markandya, A. and Barbier, E. (1989) *A Blueprint for a Green Economy.* London: Earthscan Publications Ltd.

Plant, R. (1991) *Modern Political Thought.* Basil Blackwell.

Rawls, J. (1988) *A Theory of Justice.* Oxford University Press.

Rosenblum, N.L. (Ed.) (1989) *Liberalism and the Moral Life.* Harvard University Press.

Scruton, R. (1984) *The Meaning of Conservatism.* Macmillan.

Shoard, M. (1987) *This Land is Our Land.* Paladin.

Part Two

Practical Applications

Community arts

Peter Bramham

This chapter provides an introduction to the distinctive issues and debates that constitute the theory and practice of 'community arts' in the UK. The nature, scope, and future of community arts have been and remain crucial ingredients of the context in which artists have found themselves working. It is no easy task to define community arts as a social movement, in terms of policy, or in terms of artistic practices. Those concerned have been reluctant to reflect upon the precise nature of 'community arts'.

It is important to grasp some of the distinguishing features that would help to demarcate community arts from other aspects of work in local communities. A diversity of theories and practices surround community arts, the role that the arts and artists can play within local communities, and their distinctive contributions to wider processes of political and cultural change.

This chapter is divided into several sections. The starting point is to provide a working definition of what is meant by community arts by examining the complex nature of its two constituent concepts – 'art' and 'community'. The next section examines the policies and practices surrounding the history of the community arts movement and its subsequent funding, initially by the Arts Council of Great Britain. This history highlights the divergent and developing philosophies and practices of community artists and how these in turn relate to the wider political, social, economic, and cultural contexts within which community art has developed. There is a need to explore the contribution that the community arts movement has made towards debates about social policy, society and politics. The penultimate section examines the contribution that arts in communities can make towards active citizenship and democracy. The final section studies the changing policy contexts within which art, community artists and local communities exist within the UK.

Defining community arts

Drawing from the discussion of 'community practice' in Chapter 1, we may characterize a community approach to the arts as embodying the following principles:

- A commitment to working collectively, with providers and clients as partners in the process of identifying and meeting artistic and social needs.
- An acknowledgement of the value of community resources in the development and creation of art processes and products.
- A recognition of the idea of 'community' as a spatial locality, as a social network and system of shared values, as an interest group, as representing cultural and religious attachments, and so on.
- An emphasis on meeting the cultural/recreational needs of those least likely to benefit from or engage with market-orientated or traditional public-sector arts provision; minority, special interest and disadvantaged social groupings are therefore given priority.
- An awareness that participation in the arts may contribute to community development and be a means of community action, leading to change.

Having provided a clarification of the nature of

community practice, we must define the nature of the arts and artistic practices. Most commentators have a reasonably clear understanding of what constitutes 'art' – starting from the traditional fine arts, such as painting, sculpture, dance, music, drama and literature, and moving to modern, more popular forms of photography, jazz and cinema. Each artistic practice has its own history, mediated by critics, with key artists and works of art. Schools of thought surround the nature of art, the importance of form and content, style, technique and the significance that particular art forms or practices hold for the development of art. The arts speak in a language that transcends locality and nationhood. One can talk about a broadly based European heritage of art, with distinct historical periods and developments. It has been and still is an exclusive and imperialist tradition, and it is the traditionally excluded that community arts seek to address.

Given the two working definitions of both community practice and arts, one way forward is to superimpose the two concepts to offer the generic term 'community arts'. Most definitions of community arts start with the interface between certain artistic practices and local communities. In contrast to the traditional arts (where the focus is narrowed down to the aesthetic defined within national and transnational cultures), community art lives on the interface between artistic practices based in local communities and their relation to the wider society. The Baldry Report (1974) shied away from an essentialist definition of community arts but underlined the distinctive position that community art takes towards its own practices and their capacities to engage members of local communities. It is possible to go beyond Baldry's evasion by denoting the family resemblances, and the major uses of the term community arts to describe particular practices.

Table 4.1 Comparing community arts and traditional arts

	Community arts	Traditional arts
Focus	Local	National/international
Cultural forms	Popular	High/fine arts
Artistic rationale	Extrinsic – art as a means	Intrinsic – art as an end in itself
Artistic practices	Murals, festivals, video, photography	Ballet, opera, drama, classical music
Sites	Streets, parks, community centres, shopping malls	National galleries, local authority museums, private collections
Artistic emphasis	Participation process	Performance product
Art/society relationship	Integrated with everyday culture	Distinct from everyday culture

Tables 4.1 and 4.2 (p. 91) seek to delineate the polarities between traditional and community-based art. This broad brush approach invites criticism and should not close minds to thinking about clear exceptions that occur on the ground to such sweeping categorizations.

'Democratization of culture' and 'cultural democracy'

The basic demand from the community arts movement is one for cultural democracy rather than the democratization of culture. The two major policy differences are as follows. A strategy for the democratization of culture suggests that there exists a discrete body of art and cultural heritage, often national in scope, which must be shared. These works of art, literature, music and dance are complex, universal and of the highest quality. Certain groups in society experience barriers such as lack of opportunity, material resources, ignorance, etc., which can be overcome by education. The democratization of culture envisages that the highest qualities of art, usually associated with national elites, can percolate and be diffused into the lower reaches of civil society.

In contrast, the policy of cultural democracy challenges the elitism within the democratization of culture strategy. Cultural democracy celebrates the variety of tastes, which sustain a plethora of cultural forms. There are no universal criteria to distinguish one artistic form as inherently superior to others. The advocates of the democratization of culture tend to focus on more traditional national art forms and artifacts, whereas defenders of cultural democracy highlight the rich variety of cultural forms. Cultural democracy opens up neglected and hidden cultural and artistic activities as worthy of serious evaluation and public subsidy. Kahn (1978) detailed the diversity of arts within ethnic minorities such as the Bangladeshis, Chinese, Cypriots, East and Central Europeans, Pakistanis, Indians, West Indians and Africans. She argued that ethnic minority arts made a substantial contribution to UK culture. Arts and race policies neglected or ignored the carnivals, dance, drama, music, festivals of ethnic communities, and cultural forms integral to ethnic identity and solidarity.

Art, animation and access

Walters (1989, p. 62) suggests two types of community-arts practice: the *animateur* model and the community model. As an *animateur*, the professional community artist is a catalyst; in the community model the *animateur* is invited in by grass-roots community organizations for advice and support. In practice differences are empirically less clear and revolve around the degree of empowerment of the local community and its control over policy. Walters uses the Craigmillar Festival to illustrate how neighbourhood workers guided both policy and professional directors, financed by Council of Europe money.

The three major features of community arts are art, animation and access. Rather than developing new art forms, artists have focused upon a variety of techniques of working with people in local communities. Co-operative and collective methods and processes of working have been central to working with a variety of groups, including children and adults, people with special needs, as well as disadvantaged target groups conventionally associated with social policy – the unemployed, racial minorities, women, the elderly and the institutionalized. Often working from arts or resource centres, community artists have in general sought to transcend middle-class audiences of amateur arts and have been interested in making some impact upon local communities, to increase creativity, self-determination, and local identity, and to enrich community consciousness and empower localities.

One important strategy, then, in community arts is animation, with artists working to develop often latent creative needs in local community settings. Mennell (1979) draws a distinction between three levels of needs within cultural policy – manifest, latent and real needs. Much policy focuses on manifest or expressed needs, with policy-makers providing services in response to existing demand or wants. By way of contrast, animation calls for policy-makers to explore people's latent needs, perhaps through taster sessions, in-depth qualitative interviews, and extensive community audits and surveys, with democratic styles of service delivery. Such strategies are more resonant with proactive innovative cultural policies in France than with the more staid reactive service delivery symbolic of UK social administration. Community artists seek to bring in and impact upon individuals as people rather than to treat them as subjects, clients or consumers. They seek to make art less remote and more relevant to people's everyday lives, to build on a diverse and vibrant amateur arts tradition. If traditional arts may be symbolized by portraits of historic figures. painted by famous artists, hanging in national galleries, community arts may be signified by face painting – a more transitory experience, with the person choosing the style and colours and marvelling in the different faces of other people in the community festival.

The community arts, then, are associated with certain distinctive artistic practices, which can be loosely caricatured as an innovative bricolage of art, crafts, sports and drama. These different forms coalesce often into community festivals or local events, with a major emphasis on participation, collective co-operation and fun. Consequently, the community arts are most clearly associated in conventional wisdom with mural painting, community photography, creative game sessions, printing, newsletters, drama, video projects and so on. These different techniques often focus around timetables, histories, places, and events that have local significance.

Finally, community arts emphasize access and accessibility. On the whole they are democratic and inclusive in outlook, with a local base. To label such art amateurish is problematic and contentious. The distinction between professionals and amateurs in some areas of arts activity, including many of the arts activities of ethnic minorities, is inappropriate or irrelevant. Community artists as *animateurs* combine their individual professional careers (in dance, music, literature) with community projects and amateur initiatives. Hutchinson and Heist (1991, p. 10) suggest that rather than a clear divide there is a complex amateur/ professional continuum or spectrum of ambition, accomplishment and activity. Community artists encourage amateurs in local communities to have the competence and confidence to produce and to consume their own artistic and cultural practices. This stands in stark contrast with the traditional arts, which have historically been the prerogative of elites and an arts establishment, performed by professionals for consumption by metropolitan, national and international audiences. See Table 4.2

To conclude by way of definition:

> The term refers to the activity of artists in various art forms working in a particular community, and involving the participation of members of that community... By involving the public in the creative process they (community artists) recognize a widespread need for creative expression in society and seek to remove the feeling that art is something remote, something irrelevant to the ordinary process of life (ACGB quoting Clark, R. (1988) *Art, Patronage and Equity*).

This conventional and harmonious picture of community arts, celebrated by the Baldry Report (1974), has its critics, some of whom have been involved with the community arts from their inception. Owen Kelly (1984) has suggested that this definition of the community-arts movement may have captured the major aspects of the movement in the 1970s but, with increased funding from the central and local state, those connected with the community arts have lost sight of the important interface between art, local communities and any radical position with regards to art and to wider social processes such as class, sexuality or race. During the 1980s community arts secured their own niche within the conventional wisdom of the arts establishment.

In the 1970s murals depicted local people, often the artists themselves, and were collectively designed expressions of local identities. In the 1990s murals have been commissioned from professional artists

Table 4.2 A comparison of community arts and traditional arts policy

	Community arts	Traditional arts
Policy rationale	Pluralism cultural democracy	Elitism democratization of culture
Policy focus	Devolution empowerment	Conservation of national heritage
Policy mediation	Animation	Education
Artistic role	Professional advice/animation of amateurs	Professional performance
Artistic needs	Latent	Established tastes
Artistic message	Local	Universal
Artistic ownership	Local/neighbourhood	Private/nation state
Artistic production	Collective	Individual genius
Audience	Ordinary people	Cultural elite artistic critics
Artistic participation	Inclusive	Exclusive

designed to 'give a competitive edge to a city... (the arts) act as an asset in the city's industrial and residential growth and add a creative dimension to a region, providing it with distinction and prestige' Myerscough (1989).

For example, a substantial mural signifying Manchester's history includes portraits of actors from *Coronation Street*, as if they were real people. Kelly's polemical book argues that community artists have become the lackeys of state quango funding and have failed to criticize wider social arrangements, while allowing themselves to drift into professionalization and incorporation into state agencies. They have become rebels, licensed by the state; the community-arts movement as a whole is deemed guilty of liberal pragmatism, addicted to state policies and funding.

Community arts as policy

This section traces the development of community arts through the history of community arts policies and the politics of arts funding. Many of those in the community arts movement grew out of what Martin (1981) terms the expressive revolution of the 1960s – a cultural sea change in attitudes, values, beliefs, which found its expression within youth cultures, music, tastes and lifestyles. In the 1960s community arts groups matured along with diverse anti-establishment movements – the underground press, free festivals, anti-nuclear groups, feminism, spiritualism, alternative medicines and technologies, environmentalism, yippees, Black Panthers, communes and others. Traditional practices and conventions were subject to revolutionary challenges and changes. Art and art forms were no exception. Art and the place of art in people's lives were felt to be too narrowly defined. The traditional pattern of public subsidy from the Arts Council had been conservative, supporting national companies and national heritage in arts, drama and opera. Nevertheless, sections within the Arts Council of Great Britain (ACGB) did recognize a range of new initiatives, projects and new groups; they sought a means to fund them without offending the entrenched interests of the more traditional establishment of the ACGB. During the early 1970s the Association of Community Artists (ACA) proved to be an influential lobbying group and provided an important fillip to the community arts movement. It gradually became more of a consumer pressure group, which demanded increased state funding, less bureaucracy and more freedom for grant-holders.

The ACGB sanctified community arts by building upon ACA definitions and receiving its Directory (submitted by the ACA, listing 149 groups and in addition fourteen individuals), thereby legitimating certain groups and artistic practices as community arts projects 'with potential'. Historically what counted as community arts projects were those projects funded by the ACGB as community arts. Critics felt that the community arts movement had begun to lose its way and had set off down the long road to incorporation and control by the state.

The Baldry Report evaded defining community art as any particular aesthetic practice but rather defined it as an approach to the relation between art and society. It was further characterized by a commitment to animation and popular involvement, using a variety of techniques. The ACGB working party was keen not to offend the traditional views of the arts establishment, which had hitherto concentrated its funding on 'centres of excellence' within a reasonably narrow range of the arts. It had avoided the thorny problem of defining what constituted art and proceeded to legitimate community arts by relating community art initiatives to Clause 3 of the original charter of the Arts Council. By so doing, the working party members, who were in general sympathetic to the aims of the community arts movement, secured public funding for community arts projects. They also succeeded in avoiding hostility from centres of symbolic power in the national arts lobby, associated with traditional arts funding and public subsidy.

In the mid-1970s the ACGB implemented the Baldry Report by setting a community arts panel and appointing a community arts officer. The community arts movement started with a budget of £176,000 in 1974–75, allocated to fifty-seven projects, which increased to £350,000 in the next year for seventy-five projects. The funding for community arts remained stable during the decade. However, the budgets for community arts projects were gradually devolved to the Regional Arts Associations. At that particular time there were growing concerns within the arts establishment that certain community arts groups were too political, i.e. that the boundaries between art and politics were being blurred. Given the commitment of community artists to challenge the place of art and culture within present society, it was perhaps not so surprising that the ACGB should wish to distance itself from more controversially radical community arts groups.

The funding process was not all one way. Funding agencies demanded reports, constitutions, evaluations of expenditure; and working relations between community arts groups and funding officers developed. Many radical community groups became heavily dependent upon mainstream funding – from central government, the Arts Council, local authorities, and charitable trusts such as the Calouste Gulbenkian Foundation. Such financial support permitted funding agencies to set their own agenda and put pressure upon community arts groups to respond to shifts in policy agendas.

The important question remains – why should government finance the arts and why community arts? The arguments against state subsidy for the arts can be found in the Adam Smith Institute's *The State of the Arts*, which favours market forces to allocate resources to sustain art and artists. The arguments for public subsidy can be found within Arts Council publications. From the outset, one clear rationale can be found in the ACGB's annual report 1975–6, *The Arts in Hard Times*. The ACGB's chair, Lord Gibson, saw community arts as a grass-roots movement increasing access to the traditional areas of Arts Council funding – drama, ballet and opera – so as to open up works of cultural heritage, housed in national galleries to new community groups. A powerful educative function was allotted to the community arts in addition to its democratic credentials of animation and participation. Another important factor was that the government felt it had to respond to the sheer explosion of community arts projects. Public funding increased the visibility of community arts, with more groups emerging to compete for public subsidy. At the same time a new wave of artistic and cultural experts were co-opted on to Arts Council panels and were keen to support new initiatives and projects within the arts world.

Community arts and social policy

Having just managed to gain public subsidy for community arts projects (notably the Quality of Life Experiments in the early 1970s), the community arts movement was immediately confronted by rapid change in the guise of wide-ranging policy debates about the crisis of the welfare state. The shifts in policy debates about public expenditure have been fully explored elsewhere (Henry, 1993), with Coalter (1989) describing the shift in public policy from recreational welfare to recreation as welfare. What did become clear was that the demands for universal welfare services for all citizens belonged in the past. Given financial restrictions on public expenditure and stagflation, welfare services would be increasingly selective, focusing upon target groups defined as those being most in need.

Given the commitment of community artists to make the arts more accessible to a wide range of social groups ignored by more traditional arts, it is not surprising that community arts were closely associated with a host of disadvantaged groups. The latter became target groups that became of increasing interest to policy-makers during the 1970s as the problems and weaknesses in welfare-state provision became increasingly obvious. The DoE encouraged community arts initiatives to ease graffiti, and to bring children into community projects to liven up drab and deteriorating inner-city housing estates. Social policy-makers and gatekeepers turned their attention to urban deprivation, defining priority areas in need of state intervention. Community arts were felt to be the ones that built communities, ones that contributed to the quality of people's lives.

Within this shifting policy context during the late 1970s and early 1980s community arts organizations worked increasingly with designated disadvantaged groups – the unemployed, the handicapped and the institutionalized – particularly the elderly. Organizations such as Graeae, Amici, Hospital Arts and SHAPE built reputations for working with the disadvantaged. Community arts became closely linked with community care, and welfare arts programmes added an important dimension to funding criteria. One such policy area was people with special needs and the publication of the Attenborough Report (1985) represented a symbolic milestone to increase disabled people's connection with the arts as participants and as part of the audience. The Carnegie Review Council (1989) reviewed the little headway made since the original report. Policy debates throughout this period began to recognize the persistence of what seemed intractable problems of inner-city decline, and youth unemployment, especially among racial minorities. The cities of Sheffield and Stirling, for example, encouraged community arts to deal with urban problems such as graffiti and underage drinking. In the quest for funding, both from the central and local state and from charitable organizations, community arts groups came under increasing pressure to legitimate their own work in terms of social relevance to wider policy goals.

In one sense community arts were strategically located to win resources at this particular time. Many of the policy debates were about the decentralizing and democratization of public services, and, at the same time, art and artistic practices were not a central part of the political discourse surrounding issues of individual and collective consumption, unlike other community groups, which organized around housing, education, and neighbourhood amenities. In that sense community arts, unlike other activist groupings, appeared to be less partisan and less critical of the wider debates surrounding economic and social policy. It was precisely this capacity to assume agendas set by funding agencies that so disturbed Owen Kelly. He berated the community arts movement in the 1970s and 1980s for being seduced by the target group discourse and by priorities set by finding agencies, without carrying a discrete agenda of its own. However worthy the target groups were, it simply was not possible to take state money and run.

Community arts and urban politics

Many commentators on the left, such as Stuart Hall, Andrew Gamble, John Hargreaves and Paul Willis, were fearful of the underlying rationale behind the policies of central government and its growing commitment to policies for community development and social integration. Throughout this period academic commentators debated the concept of social control, and many community initiatives were described as subtle forms of social control. One of the many outcomes of the riots in Brixton in 1981 was the appointment of a community artist to the area. Some community projects were funded by the Manpower Services Commission's community programme, which was primarily concerned to deal with youth unemployment and provide training and work experience.

At the beginning of the 1980s this debate was further complicated with the arrival of the new urban left in the Labour Party, eager to introduce a new form of local politics. Such urban politics sought to create new alliances with community groups and to be more responsive to local interest groups. Arts and cultural policies were to play an increasing role in this new urban politics. Given the decentralization of community arts funding to Regional Arts Associations, community arts groups were drawn into closer working relations with regional bodies and local authorities rather than the national ACGB. During the early 1980s there were attempts by socialist-led local authorities, particularly metropolitan counties and the Greater London Council (GLC), to generate urban 'rainbow coalitions' with new social movements – feminist groups, racial minorities, environmental/consumer groups, and gay and lesbian groups.

The GLC arts strategy was to question arts culture and develop stronger links with local community groups. Between 1981 and 1986 the GLC spent more than £10m. through the Community Arts and Ethnic Subcommittees, as well as supporting popular initiatives through the Arts and Recreation Programmes. With an initial budget of £1m., the Community Arts Committee and the Ethnic Minorities Committee became the formal channels to build bridges with the previously powerless and neglected groups. Arts and cultural policies were seen as crucial ingredients of empowerment, of signifying discrete identities and providing support for previously 'invisible' groups. There was a growing realization of the need to acknowledge the diversity within inner-city communities and developing multicultural policies that did justice to the history and vitality of diverse cultural forms.

The 'white' selective tradition within Arts Council policy had already been highlighted and criticized by the writing of Kahn (1976) and Owusu (1986). Cultural traditions from diverse ethnic identities became crucial ingredients in local communities seeking to resist racism and to construct a positive black image and history through community arts. Bianchini (1987) and Mulgan and Worpole (1986) provide a detailed analysis of the development of GLC arts policies and the uneasy relations developed with particular groups. Although the GLC became increasingly aware of the need to develop popular cultural forms and work with market forces rather than against them, the strategy concerned itself more with arts consumption than with an arts-industries or production strategy.

Research to examine how successful its strategy was for broadening the base for the arts was commissioned by the GLC. The research used focused population surveys in three working-class areas – Deptford, Brixton and Dalston, user surveys at a range of venues, group discussions with regular users and interviews with community arts project workers. From the surveys 40 per cent could name the community arts project in their area and the same percentage had attended some community art event during the past 12 months. One in eight of those surveyed (ss=900) had had some connection with a community arts project, including women, black groups and the unemployed. Little difference was to be found in the characteristics of 'regular' and 'casual' users of community arts projects. Yet community arts audiences displayed some similar characteristics to traditional arts audiences. Class and education were still crucial divisive factors in participation rates; the middle class and educated exhibited double the rates of involvement in community arts, overriding such other factors as gender and unemployment.

The GLC acknowledged the possibility of art and culture providing the means to build a political (in this case socialist) message. The GLC was led by a new generation of politicians who sought to restructure the party and redress the declining support for the Labour Party from the traditional trade-union movement and the older generation of more right-wing labour activists. This strategy demanded developing links and broader bases of support than traditionally had been the case within labour organizations. Community arts projects had attracted two types of oppositional groups – middle-class Labour voters and working-class groups that ignored partisan politics. Local community groups began to look to the GLC as an important source of funding rather than part of the local state that was responsible for inadequate services in the fields of education, housing, amenities, etc. This change in outlook was slow to achieve and can be overstated, yet many community-based groups were drawn into funding arrangements with the GLC, and community arts projects were no exception.

The successes of the GLC initiatives have been evaluated, particularly in terms of their economic strategy (McIntosh and Wainwright, 1987). It is worthwhile noting that emphasis was laid on the policy process rather than on the outcomes. Such an emphasis has been part and parcel of community arts strategies and techniques. The GLC did commission research on the impact of community arts and on the nature of community arts audiences. Drawing on case studies of the Metro, Rio, Albany Empire, Centreprise and Tower Hamlets arts projects, the researchers found that community arts participation was essentially the preserve of 22–30 years olds, particularly the well educated. Despite several attempts to develop a broad-based community approach, many projects brought together young middle-class Labour supporters. In terms of the cultural politics of the new left such an outcome was unintended; traditional social filters and symbolic boundaries persisted in excluding target groups, even in the community arts.

The GLC cultural and arts policies provide something of a watershed in policy terms. The GLC provided an exemplar of how the new left could use the local state to generate new policies and new policy communities. Other local authorities watched what was happening in the metropolis and attempted to apply and adapt such policies to their own local constituencies. The successes of the new left have been mixed and are sanguinely evaluated by Lansley *et al.* (1989). Nevertheless, for the first time, politicians began to look towards a particular kind of arts policy as part of cultural politics. The main ingredients of cultural politics are those of decentralization, democratic representation and providing access for disadvantaged groups to the means of cultural and symbolic production. This has meant being drawn into cultural industries strategies and funding sites of popular culture and music that previously were solely supplied by market forces. Manchester and Sheffield have embarked upon different versions of cultural industries policy, and both cases symbolize a major shift in arts policy from the democratization of culture towards cultural democracy.

Community arts, participation and citizenship

Policy-makers, academics and practitioners have been reluctant to discuss what constitutes good community-arts practice. In fact there has been little theoretical debate to evaluate the success or failure of practices within projects. This silence cuts little ice within policy communities that demand objective performance indicators, value for money and customer satisfaction. Community art as a label does not so much describe what is done and by whom but rather why it is done.

From its inception community art has been defined much more by what it was not than what it was. It was not established art – the traditional world of national or metropolitan culture so clearly painted by Hutchinson (1982) and depicted in the phrase 'the making of the opera class'. The community arts movement stood initially for activism and participation. It sought to avoid traditional art forms, which were redolent with class distinction and reduced people to passive consumers, spectators of professional performances.

The driving rationale and conventional wisdom of the community arts movement have been about animation and participation. During the 1970s one apocryphal story of the vagaries of Arts Council subsidy was one of funding three people to walk between villages in East Anglia wearing bowler hats and balancing a plank on their heads. In reality, they were part of a community arts project that comprised children's animation, games, storytelling, puppetry and the like. Once they arrived in outlying villages, the walkers set about organizing a variety of local events to encourage community participation and development.

Community arts practice has sought to work in and with communities. In contrast to traditional arts funding, which has concentrated on performances and exhibitions at prestigious art venues, theatres and concert halls by professional companies, community arts groups have tended to be engaged in longer-term projects and events. This has been developmental work to encourage the participation of those in communities in a range of artistic practices and aesthetic experiences. The events tend to be local in character and use community resources such as community centres, schools, parks, playgrounds, streets and open spaces rather than purpose-built centres for art, music and drama. These activities then take place at particular times as events are linked to different places and carry historic, symbolic and ethnic significance for individuals and collective groups living locally. Local people are co-participants in the artistic enterprise and empowered by it.

The strategies for funding community *animateurs* and developing careers in community arts have been varied. Some community artists have received salaried commissions from both the public and private sectors to live within particular communities and to encourage local participation in a particular art form. As workers, community artists have collectively discussed the need to affiliate to trade unions, and to create professional associations capable of providing training and professional accreditation for practitioners. Sponsorship briefs have often been linked to work with disadvantaged target groups, such as women, ethnic minorities and the elderly. Critics of such initiatives point out that artists have been in the community but were not of the community. They have been usually white middle class and have been assigned to multi-racial, working-class communities, often at the margins of urban inner city life.

In contrast to the salaried individual with particular technical skills in conventional art forms, plus an open-ended commitment to animation, many community artists were of the community; they belonged to and were funded by local community groups. These co-operative community-arts groups have toured the regions with socially relevant and local materials – often reconstructing key historical events of local significance, or addressing key topics around the position of women, racial minorities and so on, while encouraging audience participation.

The issue of audience participation with the commitment to animation introduces the notion of authorship and creativity. Many community artists have stressed the importance of creative involvement in artistic processes and the collective nature of such involvement. This has shifted the focus of artistic practices away from the unique creativity of one particular artist, composer, etc., towards art and artistic practices as shared collective projects with no authoritative voice. in contrast to rigid hierarchies of masters, apprenticeships and the like, community arts offer a more democratic, open-ended commitment to art. Some critics of this approach have detected declining standards, suggesting that the commitment to process devalues the artistic outcomes. The central emphasis on process can also be tied into the broader commitment to effect social change, engage in political action, and promote environmental and cultural changes.

Given its roots in direct democratic action and citizenship, the community arts movement has had to come to terms with policy makers and professionals mediating artistic practices. Some community arts groups refused to accept Arts Council funding, seeing it as state support and possible censorship on freedom to engage in political comment and critique. Many were concerned about the incorporation of community art within mainstream ACGB funding and the capacity of sponsors to set agendas and provide professional career paths for community artists. Some demanded alternative ways of funding community arts so as to avoid reliance upon revenue grants, with a view to creating closer links with local communities within which artists were working.

The role of professionals within leisure organizations within the voluntary sector is a major theme in the work of Bishop and Hoggett (1985). They are fearful of the local-authority professionals attempting to manage and organize leisure enthusiasts. Many of the themes in Bishop and Hoggett's work relate directly to the philosophy of community art practices. They characterize the leisure groups as essentially democratic organizations that provide mutual aid to fellow members, who produce and consume their own goods and services. They are essentially local in character and provide one of the few contexts within modern industrial societies where individuals can creatively express and organize themselves. For Bishop and Hoggett leisure groups within the voluntary sector are general expressions of what the community arts movement is primarily concerned with – providing open democratic access for people to become creative members, and to produce and consume art and aesthetic experiences. Goods, services and experiences are mediated by non-market processes.

The limited research that has been completed into the community arts highlights the importance of local networks that lead to people's involvement with community arts projects. In one survey of users, 49 per cent had heard of the community arts project by word of mouth and a further 29 per cent had literally walked past the project venue and had come in to explore what was going on. Such findings highlight the importance of local 'mental maps' in people's everyday lives and the informal barriers that may characterize community arts projects. There are, then, a range of clues and signposts which signify whether people feel at ease in community arts settings – the choice of food, the friendly or unfriendly atmosphere of venues, the particular activities and programmes on offer. Many people were put off by issues surrounding political correctness of styles of life, the cultural politics of food, the content of arts programmes, and so on. Much advertising, for example, tended to be directed at people already inside the arts. Those 'in tune' with projects will colonize places and projects, and in so doing exclude others.

Bishop and Hoggett draw in part on the work of Anthony Cohen and cultural anthropology in suggesting that people occupy symbolic universes. Such an approach stresses the importance of symbolic boundaries that constitute shared communities of meanings, binding people in as members. People therefore are insiders and outsiders; there are subtle boundaries of meanings that give people a sense of identity, a sense of belonging. Often these boundaries have physical dimensions, providing members with a sense of place. For Bishop and Hoggett leisure organizations provide mutual aid in leisure – they are essentially democratic and provide a sense of identity and active citizenship. For the community arts movement these essential characteristics permeate the processes of events and projects that encourage the creative participation of individuals and groups within a range of aesthetic activities and happenings. The processes create boundaries and identities, contributing to collective memories. Murals, plays and festivals celebrate locality and membership; people belong and participate in a wide variety of aesthetic experiences that celebrate collective processes and locality. Bishop and Hoggett suggest that enthusiasts enter shared symbolic universes. For community artists these shared symbolic universes focus upon a wide range of aesthetic practices, collectively shared and democratically covering a wide range of people as they satisfy both manifest and latent needs and talents.

In contrast to the established arts, the community arts movement has had the critical potential to test out the relation between art and the wider society. It has encouraged people to be active producers of art and cultural forms and to reject what Illich terms the radical monopolies set up by welfare-state professionals, who educate the public to become consumers of the existing service. Community artists have advocated democratic control over the production, distribution and consumption of cultural goods and messages.

Arts, local communities and economic change

The fierce debates about the democratization of culture and cultural democracy sound a little hollow in the 1990s. Cultural activism, especially funded by the state, appears out of date after the new realism blowing through the years of the 1980s under the broad policy banner of Thatcherism. Throughout the 1980s the Arts Council came under pressure to legitimate its policies and to delegate more responsibilities to Regional Arts Associations. The policy documents *Glory of the Garden* (1983) and the *Wilding Report* (1989) illustrate the general philosophy behind these shifts in thinking.

While quangos were re-examining their own organizational structures and modes of funding, there was growing conviction within the arts establishment of the economic significance of the arts. Industrial cities were slowly acknowledging this economic significance in revitalizing and restructuring themselves. The aesthetic and social discourse about the importance of the arts was superseded by a powerful and convincing business discourse:

> The arts stimulate growth in ancillary industries and generate hot spots of urban development. The arts act as a magnet drawing people to particular localities, where these ancillary industries can take advantage of an expanding consumer base... The arts work to improve the image of a region and can spearhead promotion... The arts are an investment in the future. They provide a source of creativity in the city with wide ramifications for enterprise and entrepreneurial activity (Myerscough, 1989).

Investing in the cultural infrastructure actually created jobs, attracted tourism and revitalized city centre areas. Many writers were beginning to discuss gentrification within UK cities, with cultural industries and sectors emerging from the ashes of industrial wastelands. For example, in Bradford old industrial workplaces such as textile mills become transformed into art galleries and sites for imaginative events. Just as Titus Salt was committed to build a planned industrial community on the outskirts of Bradford, with managed leisure and recreation, the same buildings, deprived of their original industrial use, have become the site for arts projects, and a gallery for a local and internationally famous artist, David Hockney. *West Side Story* was staged just after the opening of the Salts Mill complex, using local youngsters as cast.

The arts lobby has always acknowledged the economic importance of the arts – their contribution to international tourism, VAT receipts, jobs and so on (Baldry 1981, Walters 1989) but it was the detailed case study by Myerscough that started to put figures on the economic relevance of the arts. Myerscough for the PSI examined the economic significance of the arts in three case studies – Glasgow, European City of Culture in 1990; Ipswich; and Liverpool. These studies highlighted the multiplier effect that arts investment has upon cities and, in particular, the neighbourhoods in which they were located. There was a growing acknowledgement among local policy-makers, planners, architects and the like that arts investments and cultural centres are crucial in attracting both public and private capital.

Cities are increasingly competing with each other to offer a wide range of arts and cultural facilities so as to attract service sector jobs from the central state or multinationals to settle in their region. The policy debates explore the tensions between large-scale city-centre development as against small-scale neighbourhood-based projects. One major criticism of the art and cultural policy of Glasgow was that it funnelled investment into the city centre while stripping resources and facilities away from the working-class estates on the periphery of the city. There are also fears about a two-tier society emerging with such economic restructuring. The core of the labour force is located in service-sector jobs and has access to a wide range of arts and cultural facilities. In contrast, there are a range of unskilled and semiskilled patterns of employment, often part-time, which confine people to low income, peripheral housing estates. The urban revitalization of city centres can create culture palaces for the wealthy while the poor on the peripheries of economic and cultural life will have community arts projects.

There are real problems in cities embarking on mega projects. These projects become fusions of sports, media and broader cultural events. Roche's (1992) study of the Sheffield games highlights the tensions and problems of funding such mega events, the undemocratic *ad hoc*racy of decision-making and the legacy for local communities and later generations. In contrast, Bianchini sees a much more positive role for arts and cultural policy in order that democratic citizenship may be realized as part of the urban renaissance.

References

Adam Smith Institute (1991) *The State of the Arts.*

Attenborough Report (1985) *Arts and Disabled People.* Bedford Square Press.

Audit Commission (1991) *Local Authorities, Entertainment and the Arts.* HMSO

Baldry, H. (1981) *The Case for the Arts.*

Bianchini, F. (1992) 'Cultural Policy and Citizenship in Europe', Plenary Paper, ELRA Conference, Bilbao, Spain.

Carnegie Review Council (1989) *After Attenborough. Arts and Disabled People.* Bedford Square Press.

Bishop, J. and Hoggett, P. (1985) *Organising Around Enthusiasms.* Comedia.

Coalter, F. 'Analysing Leisure Policy', in Henry, I. P. (1989) *Management and Planning in the Leisure Industries.* MacMillan.

Henry, I. P. (1993) *The Politics of Leisure Policy.* Macmillan.

Hutchinson, R. and Feist, A. (1991) *Amateur Arts in the UK.* Policy Studies Institute.

Hutchinson, R. (1982) *The Politics of the Arts Council.*

Kahn, N. (1978) *The Arts Britain Ignores.* The Arts of Ethnic Minorities in Britain. Community Relations Commission.

Kelly, O. (1984) *Community, Art and the State: Storming the Citadels.* Comedia.

Lansley, C. *et al.* (1989) *Councils in Conflict.* Macmillan

Lewis, J. *et al.* (1986), *Art – Who needs it? The Audience for Community* Arts. Comedia.

McIntosh, M. and Wainwright, H (1987) *A Taste of Power?* Macmillan.

Martin, B. (1981) *A Sociology of Contemporary Social Change.* Basil Blackwell.

Mulgan, G. and Worpole, K. (1986) *Saturday Night or Sunday Morning?* Comedia.

Roche, M. (1992) *Identity and Citizenship.* Macmillan.

Waters, I. (1989) *Enterainments, Arts and Cultural Services.* Longman.

Further reading

Community Development Foundation (1992) *Arts and Communities.*

Keens, M. (1989) *Arts and the Changing City.* BAAA.

Owusu, K. (1986) *The Struggle for the Black Arts in Britain.* Comedia.

Community sports and physical recreation

5

Les Haywood

In this chapter we examine sports and physical recreation as an aspect of community leisure and recreation provision. In Chapter 2 we identified the defining concepts and management practices relevant to community recreation, and ended on the key point that it is necessary to go beyond these operational processes and to appraise critically the nature and values of the activities encouraged and promoted under the community banner.

Unlike community arts, which, as indicated in the previous chapter, are formally recognized by the Arts Council as areas for funding, and therefore have some form of 'official' definition, community sport and physical recreation have no such designation. Currently the label 'community' may be attached to such schemes as 'Football and the Community' or specified community groups may be targeted by 'Action Sport Schemes', but there is little if any consistency in the way the term is used. The approach we shall adopt in this chapter therefore will be to discuss those criteria that should be applied to sport and physical recreation if they are to measure up to the aims, values and methods implicit in the community practice approach – in other words, we shall initially be prescriptive rather than descriptive. The first section of this chapter will therefore be given over to a consideration of the 'ideal' dimensions of community sports and physical recreation, and then in the second section a number of case studies will be undertaken in order to assess the extent to which community sport schemes in practice match up to these ideals.

Let us begin with a number of questions about sports and their status and validity in a community context:

- Are some forms of sport better or more appropriate than others for community creation, e.g. for community development, or for benefiting specific groups?
- Are some forms of sport irrevocably flawed, and therefore untenable for purposes of community recreation, e.g. sexist, racist, class-ridden, too violent?
- Is there any place for highly developed competitive sport in community recreation? Or is community recreation, by implication, low-level, playful and anti-elitist?

In debating these questions it is important to consider different facets of the nature of sports, and the ways in which they relate to the wider social contexts in which they are situated. Sports exist at a variety of levels – from child's play to international, in a multiplicity of forms – and may be used by numerous institutions (educational, commercial, political, etc.) for their own purposes, or played just for fun and personal satisfaction. In order to untangle this complex web we shall discuss three interrelated aspects of sport and physical recreation in relation to community approaches to provision. These are:

1 The aims and objectives informing community sports and recreation.
2 The nature and structures of sports employed.
3 Issues of particular significance in the contemporary social and political contexts of sport.

Aims and objectives

Debates about the aims and objectives of sports and physical recreation have been most common in educational contexts, and in some cases have generated extensive literature and research (notably in physical education and outdoor pursuits). Despite the use of rigorous social science research methods, practitioners have generally been sceptical of the findings of such studies, preferring to apply rule of thumb judgements to their own work and often relying on tradition as the major justification for playing particular sports in particular ways. However, it is important for practitioners to scrutinize critically current practice if changes are to be made, and clearly the adoption of a community-practice approach to provision implies a questioning of what has gone before and a willingness to experiment and develop.

In assessing the aims of sports and physical recreation it is useful to consider the following question. Is sport played principally for its own sake, for immediate satisfactions, or in order to achieve aims external to the sport itself, such as health and fitness, or group solidarity and status? In other words, is sport justified instrumentally as a means to some end, or is it justified intrinsically as an end in itself? Second, we should ask whether sport is encouraged mainly for the benefits it brings to individuals, or because of benefits to society, such as a healthier workforce or the productive use of excess energy and free time.

These dimensions – means-end, instrumental-intrinsic, societal-individual – are not necessarily mutually exclusive, but they serve as a medium through which to examine the ways in which particular sorts and physical recreations are played, organized and provided. Figure 5.1 illustrates this framework for the analysis of the aims of sport and physical recreation.

MEANS		ENDS
Instrumental justification	_____	Intrinsic justification
Societal orientation	_____	Individual orientation

Figure 5.1 Aims of sport and physical recreation

Research done into the aims of physical educators (Kane, 1975) shows that they identified a variety of specific objectives in teaching sports, some of which were largely intrinsic, while others were directed at more long-term outcomes. For example, immediate objectives were concerned with the enjoyment of motor skills and self-actualization and expression through play. Instrumental, future-orientated aims included preparing for leisure and developing social and moral competencies and values.

Table 5.1 Objectives in teaching physical education

Objectives of playing	Means-Ends	Instrumental-Intrinsic	Societal-Individual	
Learning motor skills	*	*		*
Self-actualization	*	*		*
Preparing for leisure	*	*	*	*
Emotional stability	*	*		*
Social competence	*	*	*	
Moral development	*	*	*	
Organic (health) development	*	*	*	

Table 5.1 (modified from Kane) shows how different objectives for playing may be located on the continuum between MEANS and ENDS.

It should be noted that each of the dimensions represents a continuum between the two poles, e.g. between an individual and a societal orientation, and that we can only position particular aims or objectives roughly on the continuum. Furthermore it is of course perfectly possible for some objectives to be relevant to both individual and societal needs.

Conducting similar thinking in relation to community settings, we might expect sports and physical recreation agencies to be examining the potential of particular activities for fulfilling such broad aims as self-realization; co-operation and social competence; community development and cohesion. At the same time, activities whose practices imply divisiveness and unremitting competition, or violence and chauvinism, would be dismissed as lacking consonance with the community ideal. Equally, providers should seek to facilitate sports that permit the following working objectives to be achieved: open access, maximum levels of participation, high intrinsic enjoyment, emphasis on sociability, and sensitivity to diverse abilities and needs. Regrettably there appear to be few community sport and recreation providers who have begun to contemplate these issues, except perhaps for some vague anti-competitive feelings about team games and a pragmatic approach to sport for the disabled.

An exception to this neglect is to be found in the Youth Service – an area of provision more heavily biased towards education than recreation, but one that places a heavy emphasis on sports and physical recreations in its programming. Since the mid-1980s practitioners and educators in youth and community work have been debating the underlying aims and objectives of sports used in and by the voluntary and statutory youth service. For example, Marsland (1985) and Campbell (1985) have examined the potential of sports in terms of moral and social education, while Lloyd (1986) argues for the in-depth analysis of how particular sports are played and used in youth work, and calls for an assessment of the potential of specific sports to achieve desired outcomes. In a telling critique of sports whose public image is imbued with excessive competitiveness leading to violence, he says 'some sports are lost to us as youth work tools, particularly for young men... football may be one of them'. These views clearly reflect a means-orientated, instrumental justification for sports, as does that of Scott (1987), while others are critical of over-stressing instrumental and societal rationales and make a case for sports that are relatively untainted by over-seriousness if they are to be attractive and meaningful to young people, e.g. Eastwood and Buswell (1986).

It is perhaps significant that only providers with an educational emphasis to their work appear to have attempted to analyse their underlying aims and objectives, and to conduct a public debate about them. By contrast, local-authority recreation providers have largely been silent on this subject. Surely it is appropriate that they should follow the lead of the education-based agencies in scrutinizing the deeper levels of meaning of the activities they provide and/or resource under the 'community banner', if that title is to be more than tokenistic.

The nature and structure of sports

It follows from the foregoing plea for assessment and clarification of aims that we need to know more about the nature and structure of sports in order to develop a sensitivity to the exact demands and opportunities for skills, challenges and interaction available to participants in any given activity. Such analyses have been developed and include consideration of:

- Classification of the structural properties of sports.
- Activity analysis.
- 'New' games.

Each of these frameworks for analysis opens up a particular insight into the nature of sports and their potential for purposes of community recreation, and we shall consequently describe each in greater detail.

Classification of the structural properties of sports

A number of systems have been developed in order to classify such separate factors as skills, and the nature of competition and interaction in sports, (e.g. Whiting, 1975; McIntosh, 1987). A more comprehensive framework has been developed by Haywood and Kew (1984) and has been applied to the understanding of community sports and youthwork (Bramham and Henry, 1990; Kew 1987). This model examines three broad dimensions of the nature of sport forms:

(a) The characteristics of the basic *challenge* present in any given sport.
(b) The *conditions* imposed upon that challenge.
(c) The *response* resulting from the interaction of (a) and b).

The *challenge* takes one of two distinctive forms – either 'environmental' or 'inter-personal'. *Environmental* challenges are usually to do with 'playing' with gravity or friction, and may be subdivided into those posed by a natural phenomenon, such as water or snow, and those that are mainly artificial, e.g. trampolines or vaulting horses. Both types of environmental challenge may be further described as being essentially 'purposive' or 'aesthetic'. These terms

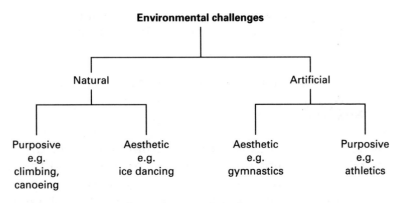

Figure 5.2 Nature of environmental challenges in sports

(adopted from Best, 1977) differentiate between those sports in which the *outcome* is central and those in which the *style* of performance is paramount. Of course style and outcome are linked in most sports, but this distinction helps to clarify the fundamental intention at the core of any particular environmental challenge, as illustrated in Figure 5.2.

The fact that many natural environmental challenge sports can easily be converted to inter-personal competitions, such as ski-racing and speed climbing, and that most artificial challenges, such as gymnastics and athletics, are usually also competitive, is acknowledged. However, the key point remains that the *primary* challenge is to overcome, individually, a problem posed by an inanimate environmental object, and only at a later and secondary stage may inter-personal competition develop; and such competition is not a component of the activity *per se*.

Inter-personal challenge sports (Figure 5.3), on the other hand, are inherently competitive, and the outcome is the goal to which all action is focused. Winning, losing and drawing are inescapable elements in the process of playing these sports. The

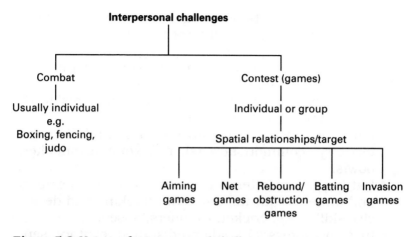

Figure 5.3 Nature of inter-personal challenges in sports

importance placed on the outcome is a matter of value – clearly these sports can be played entirely for fun or can be seen as crucial symbolic tests of individual or collective powers. What cannot be avoided is that the *raison d'être* of inter-personal sports is the comparison of skills and abilities.

These sports are of two main types, depending on the relations between the opponents: *combat* and *contest* (after McIntosh, 1963). Combat sports are essentially forms of fighting in which the objective is to strike or immobilize the opponent's body. Rules and equipment are basic and minimal, and in modern times these sports are almost exclusively individual, except for those that have degenerated into entertainments, e.g. team tag wrestling. Contest sports, on the other hand, may be individual or group activities and are much more contrived than combat sports, since they interpose various objects between the opponents, e.g. ball, bats, shuttlecocks, etc. Targets are diverse, e.g. goals, boundaries, baskets, etc., and rules are numerous and complex. A further subdivision of contest sports is possible if one examines the spatial relationships between opponents, together

with the aforementioned target. One may thus identify five distinct forms of interpersonal contest sports:

1 Aiming games (shared territory, common targets),
  e.g. golf, archery.
2 Net games (own territory to defend, opponents' territory as target), e.g. volleyball, tennis.
3 Rebound/obstruction games (shared and disputed
  territory, common targets), e.g. squash, snooker,
  bowls.
4 Batting games (alternative uses of common territory
  and targets requiring different attacking and defensive skills), e.g. cricket, rounders, baseball.
5 Invasion games (shared and disputed territory, separate targets), e.g. football, netball, basketball.

The *conditions* imposed upon the basic environmental
and inter-personal challenges have two main dimensions – equipment and regulations. The equipment
usually constitutes part of the challenge, as, for
example, in the use of racquets in badminton, and is
intrinsic to the nature of the activity; but it may also
be used as an aid or for protection, e.g. climbing ropes
or cricket pads, and is then not necessarily an essential element in defining the basic challenge.

The regulations governing sports are what ultimately
create their distinctive forms, but in most sports it is
possible to distinguish both 'canons' of acceptable
behaviour, e.g. ideas of fair play, and *rules* of necessary behaviour, which prescribe the technical requirements of how to play. All sports are also subject to the
'laws of the land', which, especially in inter-personal
sports, underpin the rules protecting players from
violent physical abuse, and may be invoked when the
rules are deliberately or recklessly ignored.

It is important to note that environmental challenges
are much more reliant on 'canons of behaviour' than
written rules, and equally that the written rules of

many inter-personal challenges are inadequate unless complemented by canons of fair play, or, at the extremes, by the wider laws of the land.

The nature of *the response* to the conditioned challenges offered by sports to individual players varies enormously from sport to sport in terms of both the psycho-motor skills and the strategies employed. Skills have been described as 'closed' or motor-dominant, and 'open' or perceptual dominant (Knapp, 1953; Whiting, 1975). Put simply, this implies that in some sports, such as gymnastics or athletics, the main concern is to perfect a series of set ('closed') motor (bodily) movements and to be able to reproduce exactly these actions at the appropriate time. By contrast, in games such as badminton or football, players learn a range of skills they are called upon to use in a changing variety of situations, and thus these skills have to be constantly adapted to cope with different conditions and problems in the moment that they arise. These activities are thus 'open', and perceptual factors are crucial elements in playing such sports. Some sports psychologists have suggested that there may be personality and cultural factors that predispose people towards predominantly 'closed' or predominantly 'open' skills, e.g. Whiting, (1975).

The foregoing classification of forms of sport is potentially important to the provider of community recreation in two ways. First, it illustrates the fact that sport is not a single, unitary phenomenon. Sports are numerous and diverse, and provide a range of different experiences, choices and opportunities. Second, it provides a means of thinking critically about the nature of different sports. In particular the model offers a tool for assessing the role of competition in sports; only inter-personal sports are inherently confrontational, for example. It can also allow a creative approach in thinking about ways in which challenges may be adapted or modified, or new ones invented, and it can help one understand social change in sports – what characteristics and properties are important in 'new' sports as opposed to traditional 'industrial' sports, some of which are in decline.

Activity analysis

Activity analysis has been developed by specialists working in the field of therapeutic recreation, mainly in the USA. It is a procedure for breaking down an activity in order to find inherent activity characteristics that can be used in devising a plan to achieve specific objectives. In the case of therapeutic recreation it is often used to treat clients suffering from particular medical disorders, but is also employed more generally in order to plan programmes of leisure activities for community groups such as elderly residents in retirement and nursing homes.

A number of methods of analysis exist, but that most commonly used (Peterson and Gunn, 1984) examines any given leisure activity in terms of its physical, social, cognitive and emotional aspects.

Physical aspects
1 Is the activity locomotor or non-locomotor?
2 Does it call for retrieval and propulsion of objects?
3 Is the movement fine motor or gross motor?
4 Which senses are stressed?
5 How much strength, flexibility, or endurance are needed?

Social aspects
1 What communication network is required?
2 Does one person receive most of the group's attention?
3 Does the activity require co-operation or competition?
4 Is physical contact required?
5 Is verbal communication necessary?

6 Can new people be met?
7 Are rewards/reinforcements available – immediately or delayed?

Cognitive aspects
1 How complex are the rules/procedures?
2 Is strategy needed?
3 Is concentration/memory important?
4 Is creative thought possible or required?
5 How structured is the activity?

Emotional aspects
What opportunities are there for expressing and experiencing emotions, such as,

1 Happiness.
2 Delight.
3 Competence.
4 Confidence.
5 Excitement.
6 Control.
7 Anger.
8 Fear, etc.

Used as an extension of the classification of sports and physical recreation, as outlined in the previous section, activity analysis provides a means of further sensitizing recreation planners to the significance of leisure activities and their potential for community use.

New games

The New Games Movement, which developed in the USA in the early 1970s, both as a recreational counter-culture to the excessive competitiveness and commercialism of corporate sport and as a means of alternative physical education, is a clear example of an attempt to devise activities consistent with values of co-operation, self-regulated competition, fun and sociability. Based on the ideas of 'soft-war' – activities that are vigorous and aggressive but avoid injury and violence, calling on the values of creativity and invention that allow games to change at will in order to satisfy the spontaneous demands of players, and emphasizing trust and co-operation rather than competition and comparison – the New Games Movement (Fluegelman, 1976) made a considerable impact on community recreation programmes in the USA and Australia during the 1970s.

Typical of the games played were 'Earthball', in which two large teams attempt to push a giant ball (6 feet in diameter) towards the opposite ends of a field, and in which players frequently change sides in order to prolong the activity; 'Infinity Volleyball', where players use standard volleyball rules, but co-operate with 'opponents' in order to keep the ball in play for as long as possible, so that the teams jointly challenge the ball and the net, rather that each other; and 'New Frisbee', which again jointly rewards the throwers and catchers of frisbees when both exhibit skilful behaviour, instead of awarding points to one or the other.

New games have been less widespread in Britain than in the USA, and indeed have been less prominent generally since the 1980s, perhaps reflecting the fact that they grew out of the now dated counter-culture that developed in the 1960s in opposition to the Vietnam War, and were heavily influenced by the 'flower children' of the hippy generation of that period. However, many of the games developed at that time are clearly consistent with community-practice ideals, and also resonate well with current values on low-cost, low-technology activities, which make few demands on environmental resources, and which are characterized by open access, making little differentiation in terms of gender, age, ability and so on.

Issues for community recreation in the contemporary social and political contexts of sport

A community approach to sports activities requires a knowledge of, and sensitivity to, issues that are of contemporary significance in the wider contexts of sports and are also matters of social concern more generally. Clearly these issues will inform our thinking about the aims and objectives discussed earlier, and will relate also to our reflections on the nature and structures of sports appropriate for community use. The relative significance of specific issues will change over time, and people's particular ideologies will affect their identification of matters of concern, but currently we would suggest the following as relevant to community recreationists:

Gender

Some sports have been criticized as being irrevocably 'gendered' i.e. so imbued with sexist (usually male) values as to render them unsuitable for an approach to participation which embraces equality as a central value. This argument would effectively eliminate a number of traditional sports from consideration. A less radical view would see the basic structure of sports as neutral in gender terms, so that any of them are potentially available to either sex, but would argue that, in order to pursue them freely, women and men should play separately, and have equal access to resources. A more liberal attitude is that adopted by the New Games advocates mentioned above, who would seek out sports that are equally available to men and women in terms of skills and participation, and do not emphasize differences in strength or agility more characteristic of males or females, or stress the complementarity of such abilities. This latter approach clearly puts a positive value on mixed activities.

Race, ethnicity and cultural pluralism

Sport has often been characterized as an area of social life in which racial and ethnic differences are less marked than in, for example, the workplace, since sport can provide a value-free framework where participation may be based on ability rather than colour. Supporters of this view point to the high representation of black players in certain sports, and to the use of sport as a means of social mobility. Opponents argue that black players are restricted in their choice of sports by racial stereotyping, and that few of them achieve central positions in mixed-race teams, or go on to become coaches and managers. Furthermore, many black children are side-tracked from other careers by the over-emphasis placed on sports by their teachers, again because of stereotyping. These matters are clearly of concern to recreation providers in multicultural environments, and attempts to provide equal access, while avoiding the pitfalls of stereotyping, are now relatively commonplace.

A further issue, however, which appears to receive little attention, is that of ethnic minority sports, and this is particularly important in the context on community recreation, which places value on the use of indigenous resources and on the recognition of cultural diversity. Most studies on race, ethnicity and sport have emphasized the issue of the access of minority groups to mainstream sports, but there is little consideration of the role of indigenous sports within specific minority communities.

Recently kabadi has been televised in Britain, and some knowledge of its significance on the Indian subcontinent has thereby become more widespread, and in some local authorities, e.g. Bradford and Leicester, facilities have been made available for local competitors. An Asian variation on volleyball is also popular in some communities in Britain, but is largely played informally with improvised facilities.

Generally, however, ethnic minority sports appear to receive scant attention compared with ethnic arts, which are widely supported in festivals promoted by local authorities, and are a recognized aspect of community arts. Clearly there is an opportunity for local-authority providers working in areas of cultural diversity to tap into ethnic community networks, in order to identify opportunities for the encouragement of sports that are representative of the cultures and traditions of particular groups, and to make them more widely available and visible.

Violence and deviant sports behaviour

'Some sports are lost to us as youthwork tools, particularly for young men... football may be one of them' (Lloyd, 1986). If providers have aims and objectives for the activities they promote in the name of community recreation, then issues such as that posed above are of central importance. Lloyd's concerns about football are two-fold: first, he sees the corrosive effects of an over-emphasis on winning resulting in a playing attitude where cheating and violence are accepted as the norm; second, football is so heavily identified with violent spectator behaviour that young people surrounded by the sub-culture of soccer are inescapably socialized into an acceptance of violence as the prime means of conflict resolution. Many other sports, and especially those where direct physical confrontation plays a part, are susceptible to criticism on the first point, although only football currently suffers the affliction of a spectator culture celebrating aggression and violence.

Community approaches to sport and physical recreation stress values of personal, social and community development, and of co-operation and respect for cultural and sub-cultural diversity and pluralism. Therefore providers are inescapably confronted with the decision either to ban activities such as football, or overtly to promote and monitor the game in such a way that deliberately sets out to counter the negative values and encourage positive ones. The existence of 'Community Football' schemes (discussed more fully below) indicates that some providers believe that football is compatible with community practice, and that it is not completely lost as an educational medium.

Elitism, commercialism and professional values

This issue is also closely linked to that of a model of sport that celebrates winning as the be all and end all of playing, and inherently downgrades the role of sports as worthwhile intrinsically, irrespective of outcome. Sports are of course inherently competitive in the sense that they all imply a challenge. However, meeting that challenge and then abandoning it, winning or losing, is the essence of sports played for their own sake. This intrinsic model of sport, charactierized and sometimes caricatured as the 'amateur ideal' was most influential in the late nineteenth and early twentieth centuries in Britain, and is still reflected in the rules of most sports, using terms such as 'fair play', 'gentlemanly conduct' (sic), etc. The problems the amateur idealists of the 1880s and 1890s encountered in maintaining their 'pure' version of sport are still present a century later. In simple terms these are two-fold.

First, there are the problems internal to sports themselves. One is a tendency to prolong the challenge beyond a single encounter in order to make lasting, rather than temporary, comparisons with others. This leads to leagues, tables, return matches and so on, and inevitably increases the value placed on victory by according it continuing significance. When in 1895 the game of Rugby football split into the two forms of

'Union' and 'League', it was as much a dispute about whether to establish league competitions or maintain simply one-off encounters, as about whether players should be paid for time lost from work when they travelled to and played matches. The latter, the issue of incipient paid professionalism, remains a problem for Rugby Union 100 years on, but leagues are now an accepted and widespread, though recent, phenomenon.

Second, there are the problems external to sports. The growth of spectatorship and the use of the popularity and visibility of sports has led people to promote issues, causes and products not directly related to the activities *per se.* These tendencies are not necessarily harmful in themselves, but their combined effect is to increase the importance of the consequences of playing at the expense of the process of playing. Spectatorship leads to 'monetization' of sports (Dunning and Sheard's inelegant term, 1977), which permits the onset of professionalization, the buying and selling of players and the growth of 'secondary producers' of sport such as coaches, managers and administrators and owners. The use of sports to promote issues and causes leads to the association of tribalism, territorialism and nationalism with sport, which at the extremes perverts a 'natural' loyalty to school, community or country into a force that loads the result of a match with a symbolic significance for players and supporters far in excess of its actual importance as a game.

The growth of the newspaper industry during the same period as the rapid institutionalization of sport saw the beginnings of a symbiotic relation between the media and sport, which fed on and developed the 'spectatorial' version of sports. Indeed newspapers were some of the first commercial sponsors of sport, acting as promoters of events in order to provide copy for their sports pages.

The development of radio and television, and thus of a truly mass media, has heightened the importance of the spectators' image of sports, at the expense of the players', and has exacerbated the tendency towards the use of sports as a vehicle for chauvinism and nationalism. At the same time of course television has made possible an exponential growth in the commercial sponsorship of sports during the past 30 years, and the massive use of the sports spectacle not only to promote issues and causes but also to sell products.

Taken together, these external uses of sports have created conditions in which some sports have become a commodity to be brought and sold, and have become highly professionalized, so that the interests of the sponsors and players are focused primarily on success – since rewards for winning far outweigh those for losing, or simply playing the game. It is under such pressures, economic and psychological, that the 'amateur ideal' begins to break down, to be replaced by a more cynical approach, in which 'gamesmanship' and 'professional fouls' are acceptable. Equally the intrinsic tendency within sports to develop and prolong the challenge adds to the importance of winning, and this always leads to elitism, since only the ruthless selection of the best available players ensures the possibility of victory.

The logic that drives modern sports, then, is inescapably one in which the end easily becomes more important than the means, the product more relevant than the process of playing. This logic is of course most apparent at the highest performance levels, but such is the persuasiveness of the mass media that their professionalized spectatorial model comes to be received as *the* dominant image in sports. If sports are to be celebrated as worthwhile for themselves, simply for the intrinsic reward of playing, and if the means of playing is to be seen as a vehicle for the promotion of positive values of fair play, co-operation and friendly competition, and the concept of community recreation demands that they should, then it is incumbent on community-sports providers and organizers to distance themselves form the excesses of professionalized sports. This could be accomplished in a number of ways, including:

- The discouragement of leagues, and tables, and the encouragement of 'one off' encounters.
- The selection of sports in which the rules emphasize co-operation and teamwork rather than individuality.
- Deliberate stress on participation at the expense of performance, e.g. modifying rules in order to include maximum participation of players, as in New Games such as multi-touch volleyball, in which the ball *must* be passed a number of times by one team before crossing the net.
- Use of sports with a low TV/professionalized profile, especially non-institutionalized activities with easily accessible skills; examples include modified hockey-'Unihoc', and short tennis.
- In sports with a high media profile, such as football, the positive encouragement of fair play and respect for opponents, and an emphasis on attacking play and taking risks rather than safe defensive methods, since the former highlights the essential process of playing, while the latter overstates the importance of the end product, the result.
- Encouragement of diversity of methods/rules within sports. For example, where governing bodies change rules to suit the result-orientated needs of TV, e.g. tie-breaks, one-service volleyball, penalty shoot-outs, etc., it should be possible to resist the spread of these changes to all levels of sport.

Community sports and physical recreation in practice

The final section of this chapter examines a number of examples of approaches to the provision of sports and physical recreation that have overtly adopted the 'community' nomenclature, in order to determine the extent to which such schemes meet the criteria outlined in this chapter, and in Chapter 2. These criteria may be briefly summarized, as follows.

General leisure policy

Nature of target groups: Disadvantaged and disenfranchised, communities of interest.

Aims of providers: Community development; community action; enhancement of quality of life for target groups.

Management style/philosophy: decentralization and localism in service provision; devolution of powers to community groups and co-participation between clients and providers; integration and partnership with other agencies.

Specific management practices: direct provision of specifically community-focused facilities; facilitation of community effort via financial and resource provision; outreach work, animation and leadership.

Sport and physical recreation policy

Aims and objectives: determination of specific 'community' aims for selected programmes and activities; evaluation of outcomes.

Selection of activities for community programmes: use of methods of analysis and classification in order to problematize the nature and structures of sport forms.

Awareness of special issues: cultural diversity/sensitivity to pluralistic needs; questioning elitism, excessive competition and violence.

Three types of provision representative of different public sector approaches will be briefly described, and subsequently their characteristics will be evaluated in relation to the above criteria.

Local-authority schemes

Many local authorities have adopted the 'community' label to describe some or all of their recreation services. However, we shall focus only on examples of those which, to varying degrees, have gone beyond the mere use of the term and have made more radical attempts to implement the community perspective in practice. All share common social and environmental conditions in focusing on inner urban areas characterized by high levels of unemployment, poor housing, relative poverty, limited space, and cultural and ethnic diversity. Initiatives on leisure and recreation in response to these conditions have taken three broad forms: direct provision, special initiatives, and comprehensive policies.

Direct provision of a community facility in an area of special need
This type of response concentrates directly on targeting provision in those inner-city areas that exhibit signs of multiple deprivation and in which recreation facilities have previously been scarce or totally absent. Power is devolved to centre managers to develop policies in consultation with local community groups and with other social service agencies working in the specific area. Efforts may be made to emphasize the localism of the centre by such measures as the recruitment of local staff, development of activity leaders from the immediate community, and deliberate under-provision of car-parking spaces in order to discourage 'commuter' usage. This type of community provision frequently co-exists alongside traditional forms of facility provision in other parts of the providing authority that are still regarded as mainstream as opposed to problem areas.

Designation of 'community recreation' as a special initiative on a city-wide basis

Here the need for a community approach is identified as existing among selected target groups across the city as a whole, rather than only in specific localities. Hence this approach is based on the use of patch workers, whose role is to reach out to communities within their designated areas in order to determine their recreational needs and to make maximum use of existing facilities – whether they be publicly owned or belong to private or voluntary organizations. Financial and other resources, such as mini-buses and equipment pools, are also provided on a city-wide basis for use by the outreach workers. Attempts are made to contact special interest groups and disenfranchized groups, and to create opportunities not previously perceived available to them, through the development of initiatives such as 'women's only' sessions.

Typically these city-wide community initiatives co-exist within the Recreation Department alongside facility and activity-based provision, and are seen in management terms as part of a comprehensive service. For example, 'community recreation' may be designated as one sub-departmental responsibility alongside those for the arts, sports and physical recreation, museums and libraries, etc. In common with the 'community-facility' approach described above, this method of working tends to identify a community perspective with social problems that can best be met by a different approach to that adopted for mainstream provision.

Community leisure and recreation as a comprehensive departmental policy

This is much more radical than the previously described ways of working, because it assumes that the community approach is appropriate to all aspects of public-recreation provision for an entire population, or at least for those sections of the population the service chooses to target. Consequently there are few examples of authorities who have gone wholly down this road, for in practice it means focusing their efforts primarily on the needs of special interest and disadvantaged groups and abandoning more general provision (or at least paying lip service to it) – a policy not conducive to winning the popularity stakes among local taxpayers. It also implies giving up some professional powers and hierarchical management systems if decentralization, devolution and consultation are practised in all areas of provision. Nonetheless one or two authorities have taken this road and have espoused the following practices on a comprehensive basis:

- Identification of selected groups and localities as the primary receivers of public recreation services.
- A shift from facility-orientation to client-orientation, and the local management of facilities (co-ownership).
- Decentralization and devolution of responsibilities within the management structure.
- An emphasis on outreach work and consultation with target groups about recreational needs.
- Questioning of the appropriateness of some traditional areas of provision, especially in the arts, parks and gardens, and museums, and to a lesser extent in sports and physical recreation.

Action sports programmes – the Sports Council national initiatives

In the 1980s the problems accruing from large-scale unemployment among young people, and the potential threat to public order posed by 'disaffected youth', gave rise to a number of specific initiatives by the Sports Council. Prominent among these were the demonstration schemes of sport for the unemployed, and the 'Action Sport' programmes targeted principally on the young unemployed in inner urban areas.

These schemes, most of which were later to pass into local-authority control, were characterized by some aspects of a community approach in that they employed 'outreach' methods as a means of contacting clients, worked in liaison with other community agencies, and promoted community participation in the leadership and development of activities. Later their remit was extended from a major focus on unemployed youth to other under-participating groups, including the elderly, disabled people, and women in general (McDonald and Tungatt, 1992).

The key findings from these demonstration projects highlighted the importance of community-based leadership and motivation, co-operation with voluntary agencies, and the value of a very specific local focus. Recognition of these factors in the *Evaluation Report on Action Sport* (Policy Studies Unit, 1986) led to the appointment of approximately 300 additional sports motivators to work with local authorities on the development of similar schemes, and financial support from the Manpower Services Commission indicated tacit central governmental endorsement for these community initiatives.

The approach to the sports activities and opportunities offered by these projects was essentially a traditional one to begin with, and football for men and keep-fit for women were the most popular, despite the provision of a much wider range of activities. Subsequently some of the schemes became more innovative by providing opportunities to sample adventure activities and expeditions in order to widen the social and sporting perspectives of young people, and a number of urban outdoor activity schemes were initiated. The adoption of adventure activities, and of fun runs and marathons, indicated that some sports leaders were aware of the importance of providing activities that complemented the lives of young people in the 'late industrial' period, and that a more critical stance to the nature and structure of sports was required if community objectives were to be met.

The underlying policy motivation behind the Action Sport, demonstration, and subsequent Sports Motivator schemes was undoubtedly a concern for social order, with the 1981 urban riots proving to be a major driving force for politicians and the Sports Council. From the beginning, then, these nationally instituted schemes had the clear aim of reducing discontent and boredom among the young unemployed. As they developed, other more expressive and less instrumental aims became apparent, such as improving the quality of life through sports participation, the values of collective community action, and the widening of horizons through adventure and expedition activities. Unlike much sports provision, where benefits are taken for granted, a number of the Action Sport schemes explicitly listed aims and objectives of the type mentioned earlier. What is unclear from the evaluation of the scheme is the extent to which the achievement of particular aims could be related to particular programmes or sport forms *per se.*

Football and the community – a partnership with the commercial sector (professional sport)

In 1978 the Minister of Sport provided a special grant, administered by the Sports Council, to provide funds for the development of what came to be called 'Football and Community Schemes'. Projects were to be developed in association with football league clubs with the joint aims of increasing the sporting facilities in urban areas and creating stronger links between the clubs and the local community. 'It was hoped by bringing fans, particularly younger ones into closer association with the club, to reduce hooliganism' (Coghlan, 1990). Funding of the initial schemes also came from the Football Grounds Improvement Trust, and subsequently what became the Football Trust (using levies largely from the football pools) has taken over financial responsibility for their continued development, while the Sports Council provides technical support.

The nature of these projects includes the provision of large sports halls, e.g. Aston Villa and Coventry City, but more usually assistance has been given to convert existing buildings for sports use, and to develop new football pitches, floodlighting of play areas, and changing facilities. By the late 1980s the partnership with the Sports Council was very limited, but the Football and the Community initiative continues, via the Football Trust, to make substantial financial contributions to local-authority schemes to improve local sporting facilities.

In practice individual Football in the Community projects have taken a number of different broadly generalized into three broad approaches:
1 Large facility schemes, which operate principally as mainstream sports-centre providers, complementing local-authority provision.
2 Football centred' projects, which emphasize the provision of football facilities and the development of schemes to encourage the playing and supporting of the game itself among young people.
3 Community-focused initiatives, which have attempted to make available more comprehensive opportunities for sports and physical recreation in the immediate neighbourhood of the football club, and have targeted a wide range of disadvantaged groups.

The last approach comes closest to the community-practice ideal. Some of the best schemes from this perspective have not only developed genuinely community-orientated sports-development schemes, but have also attempted to make the football club facilities available as a community resource, providing such as meeting rooms and drop-in centres for communal use, and allowing playing areas to be used out of season for local festivals and events, (e.g. Sheffield Wednesday and Sunderland FCs).

It is apparent that there is some tension between the 'football-centred' aims of the scheme and the 'community' intention implicit in the original proposal, and this is evident in the variety of schemes that have developed since 1978. Individual Football and the Community development officers can feel themselves squeezed between the desire of clubs to use the funds to provide what is in effect a nursery for young players and fans on the one hand, and the wider community recreation needs manifest in the inner-urban localities in which the clubs are situated, on the other.

Conclusion

It is evident that the above examples of public-sector sports and recreation provision labelled as 'community' approaches vary in the extent to which they fulfil the criteria we have set out as characterizing the community-practice ideal, both in terms of leisure policy in general, and in the approach to sports in particular. In most cases, for example, some aspects of the management of these schemes have been modified in order to allow a greater degree of local participation, and to a greater or lesser extent specific target groups have been selected for attention in all initiatives. However, few schemes pay serious attention to community development and action and to a genuine devolution of powers to community groups. In terms of the nature, structure and values of community sports *per se* few public-sector approaches have given serious thought to dealing with the question of traditional practices. This is not surprising of course in the case of Football and the Community, with its clear

Table 5.2(a) Community sport and recreation in practice – general leisure policy

Type of scheme	General leisure policy		Management		
	Target groups	Aims	Philosophy		Practice
Local authority community recreation					
Type 1 Direct provision of community sports centre e.g. Bradford	Disadvantaged disenfranchised inner-city dwellers in specific locale	Improvement of quality of life in areas of multiple deprivation. Community development	Decentralized. Some integration with other agencies		Direct provision of communally focused facility. Local staffing.
Type 2 Community recreation as a special initiative (city-wide alongside mainstream provision) e.g. Sheffield	Specific under-participating groups, e.g. ethnic minorities, women, disabled, elderly. Communities of interest	Maximizing participating opportunities	Decentralized and some devolution of powers		Facilitation via resource provision. Outreach work. Animation, leadership
Type 3 Comprehensive community recreation policy e.g. Leicester	Focus on disadvantaged, under-participating populations as *the* mainstream recipients of public provision	Redressing disadvantage. Community development and action	Decentralized: devolution of powers; some co-participation between clients and providers		Direct provision of community facilities. Facilitation via finance and resource provision. Outreach work
Sports Council 'Action Support' programmes	Initially unemployed youths in inner-city locations. Later under-participating groups – elderly, disabled, and women in general	Social control, combating boredom and discontent Improving QOL, including health and fitness	Localized control and leadership. Partnership with local authority/ voluntary sector		Facilitation via provision of resources. Outreach work. Community involvement in leadership
Partnership schemes. 'Football and the Community'	Football fans (esp. youth) in urban locations. Later extended to other residents of local league club neighbourhoods	To combat football hooliganism via community development. To maximize use of local facilities for sport	Local leadership. Partnership between Sports Council, local authority and league clubs		Facilitation via provision of resources. Some outreach work

Table 5.2(b) Community sport and recreation in practice – sport and recreation policy

Type of scheme	Sport and recreation policy			
	Aims and objectives	Selection of activities	Awareness of special issues	Comments on practice
Local authority community recreation Type 1 Direct provision of community sports centre e.g. Bradford	Maximize use by young people. Mixed motives – quality of life/social control. Improve opportunities for specific under-participating groups, e.g. Asian women, elderly	Mainly traditional group sports e.g. 5-a-side. Some encouragement of ethnic minority games/sports	Cultural diversity	Little evidence of shared control/co-operation with local community. No 'theorizing' or problematizing of sports provided
Type 2 Community recreation as a special initiative (city-wide alongside mainstream provision) e.g. Sheffield	Encouragement of under-participating groups in order to improve QOL, including health and fitness concerns	Largely mainstream sports with low skill level entry, e.g. badminton, keep fit/yoga as women's sports. Some attempts to provide outdoor/adventure activities as alternative experience	Sensitivity to pluralistic needs	Little emphasis on localism or community development. Some evidence of *ad hoc* analysis of the nature of sports
Type 3 Comprehensive community recreation policy e.g. Leicester	Sport and recreation as means of improving QOL and for community development	Focus on ease of participation; some antipathy to traditional (male) team sports; concern for 'special needs', e.g. self-defence for women; ethnic minority sports	Cultural diversity and sensitivity to pluralistic needs. Some concerns over elitism/excessively competitive sports	Equates 'community approach' almost wholly with 'disadvantaged'. Some consideration of nature and values of sports in *ad hoc* decision-making about provision, but no evidence of theorizing, or evaluation of outcomes
Sports Council 'Action Support' programmes	Maximize opportunities for people to become involved in sports and physical recreation via emphasis on leadership and motivation. Explicit aims – social control and quality of life	Initially traditional: 5-a-side football for men and keep-fit for women. Later more innovative provision of adventure facilities, fun runs, etc.	Sensitivity to pluralistic needs	Successful emphasis on local leadership and motivation, and importance of a highly specific community focus. Some attempts in specific schemes to problematize the nature of sports provided, but no effort to theorize sports or evaluate particular programmes of activities
Partnership schemes. 'Football and the Community	Initially to promote football with an emphasis on 'good behaviour'. Binding young fans to club as a collective community. Later some clubs developed role to become local sports resource	Primarily football. Some provision of other traditional/stereotyped activities, e.g. bowls for elderly	Limited	Some tension between the aims of 'football promotion' and wider community provision for sports. No overt questioning of the values of professional sports

vested interest, but it is disappointing to find self-confessedly 'experimental' schemes from the Sports Council remaining rooted almost exclusively in the past in terms of the sport forms embraced in such initiatives as 'Action Sport', with few attempts to 'problematize' or theorize them.

Tables 5.2(a) and 5.2(b) summarize the matches and mismatches between public sector 'community sports' schemes and the dimensions of community practice outlined in this chapter.

References

Best, D. (1978) *Philosophy and Human Movement.* London: Allen and Unwin.

Bramham, P. (1989) *Leisure and Urban Processes.* London: Routledge.

Campbell, C. (1985) 'Playing Seriously', *Youth in Society,* October.

Coghlan, J. (1990) *Sport and British Politics since 1960.* London: Falmer.

Dunfermline College of Physical Education (1979) *Education Outdoors.*

Dunning, E. and Sheard, K. (1979) *Barbarians, Gentlemen and Players.* Oxford: Martin Robertson.

Eastwood, P. and Buswell, J. (1986) 'Taking the lead', *Youth in Society,* March.

Fluegelman, A. (1976) *The New Games Book.* Garden City, NY: Dolphin Books.

Haywood, L. and Kew, F. (1984) 'Understanding participation in sport and physical recreation', in *New Directions in Leisure Studies,* Ilkley: BICC.

Houlihan, B. (1991) *The Government and Politics of Sport,* London: Routledge.

Kane, J.E. (1974) *Physical Education in Secondary Schools.* Basingstoke: Macmillan.

Kew, F. (1987) 'Sporting Challenge', *Youth in Society,* May.

Knapp, B. (1977) *Skill in Sport.* London: Routledge.

Lloyd, T. (1986) 'Everyone a winner', *Youth in Society*, January.

Marsland, D. (1985) 'Playing Seriously', *Youth in Society*, March.

McDonald, D. and Tungatt, M. (1992) *Community Development and Sport*, London: Sports Council.

McIntosh, P. (1987) *Sport in Society*. West London Institute.

Peterson, C. and Gunn, S. (1984) *Therapeutic Recreation Program Design*. London: Prentice-Hall.

Scott, J. (1987) 'By fair means or foul', *Youth in Society*, May.

Whiting, H. (1975) *Concepts in Skill Learning*. London: Lepus.

Community tourism

John Capenerhurst

Introduction

The joining of the term 'community' to the concept of tourism is less common than in other aspects of recreation and leisure, such as community arts and community sports, which are the subjects of the preceding chapters. No doubt the major reasons for this lie in the fact that tourism is conceived mainly as a matter for individual, rather than collective, action and choice, and that its growth in Western-style economies has been largely driven by commercial markets rather than the public sector.

However, as discussed in Part 1 of this book, There are several dimensions to the concept of community practice in leisure and recreation, in addition to an emphasis on public and collective action. Community approaches also embrace such issues as:

- A concern for the interests of local communities and interest groups.
- A recognition of cultural diversity and integrity.
- An emphasis on co-operation between providers and users, and acknowledgement of the value of indigenous resources within community groups.
- A concern for the needs of disadvantaged and disenfranchised groups.

Furthermore, as indicated in Chapter 3, although we live in a period in which market liberal economics are dominant in many spheres of social life, not the least in leisure and tourism, there are, nonetheless, several instances of market failure, which point up the need for community/state intervention in order to protect the public good and redress inequalities.

Taking these factors together, the term 'community tourism' is used in this chapter to denote two approaches within the broad field of tourism provision. The first is concerned with attempts to incorporate local community interests and a degree of community control over the nature and extent of tourism development in a specific locale – an approach in sympathy with those aspects of 'community practice' that stress indigenous resources, cultural integrity and a co-operative framework. Such initiatives have been characterized in the literature as a 'community approach', e.g. Murphy (1985) and represent a relatively familiar use of the concept. Less familiar is the second perspective employed in this chapter to denote 'community tourism', which here is conceptualized as part of a broader approach to the provision of opportunities for disadvantaged groups to participate in tourism in the interests of addressing problems of inequality and recreation deprivation. This broad approach has been described elsewhere as 'social tourism' (Teuscher, 1983). It is suggested here that as some aspects of social tourism clearly resonate with the concerns of community practice, these elements are defined as 'community tourism'.

Community tourism in general

Tourism, both domestic and international, represents a significant leisure activity in the UK and other Western democracies of Europe, North America, Japan and Australasia. In Eastern Europe there has been for many years thriving domestic tourism, a substantial amount of international travel between the countries of Eastern Europe themselves, and an increasing but minor incoming tourist trade from the West (see Buckley and Witt, 1990, for details up to 1987 on international tourist/visitor arrivals in Eastern Europe; also Davidson, 1992, pp. 164–5). It is clear, however, that most tourism is domestic rather than international; that this domestic tourism is largely confined to the rich nations mentioned above; and that international tourist movement is mainly from the prosperous nations of temperate climate to the poorer but warmer countries of the 'pleasure periphery', ranging from Mexico and the Caribbean to the Mediterranean, and from East Africa by way of the Indian Ocean and South-East Asia to the Pacific Islands (Lea, 1988, p. 1).

In the richer countries tourism has grown in importance as household real incomes and leisure time have increased. Most Northern European countries have tourism participation rates in excess of 57 per cent of population (Commission of the European Communities, 1987, in Williams and Shaw, 1988, p. 48). Eleven million package holidays from the UK were sold in the late 1980s, compared with some 5 million at the start of the decade (Urry, 1990, p. 48) and the number of overseas holidays taken by UK residents continues to rise. (Urry, 1990, p. 50).

Terms such as 'tourism', 'tourism development', 'community', are capable of a variety of meanings, according to the purposes for which the terms are used. The term 'community' has already in previous chapters been shown to be chameleon-like, and the term 'tourism' is similarly capable of a range of interpretations. In order to simplify discussion, this section on 'community tourism' will adopt the view that tourism constitutes people's travelling away from home for purposes other than remuneration and mainly for recreation, but also for conferences, visiting family or for health reasons. The definition employed here includes two groups that are sometimes disaggregated: tourists (who are usually defined as visitors making at least one overnight stop in a country or region and staying there for at least 24 hours), and the excursionist (who is a day or half-day tripper who stays less than 24 hours and does not make an overnight stop). It should be noted that for some studies the distinction is important, since tourists usually spend more money and demand more services than excursionists. Much tourism-related research is concerned both implicitly and explicitly with the tourist. Nevertheless it will be assumed in this section that the distinction is not likely to be made by the majority of a destination's residents, who will class tourists and excursionists as visitors.

'Tourism development' will be defined as the providing of or upgrading of facilities and services to meet the needs of all visitors. Clearly this kind of development can occur in a variety of forms and a variety of contexts (Pearce, 1986, p. 2). Coastal resorts, large cities, rural villages, stately homes, Disneyland, Stonehenge, National Parks, must all provide for visitors, and the ways in which the provision is carried out will constitute a particular form of tourism development. The construction of hotels, shopping malls, marinas, restaurants, ski-lifts and ski slopes, leisure centres, together with the appropriate infrastructure of roads, airports, water and sewage systems, are also part of tourism development. The sort of development will be influenced by its context: how far tourism is a major part of the economy, the wealth of a particular country, the maturity of the tourism industry, the physical environment (an inner city area, a UK National Park – very different from a National Park in New Zealand or the USA – or a Greek island). Tourism development is thus likely to be extremely varied, and so are the impacts of this development on those people who live in the development area. But impacts there will be, if development takes place, and community tourism of one kind discussed later in this chapter owes its origins, in part at least, to the concerns of residents about the form and pace of developments.

'Community tourism' is a relatively new term, which can refer to two kinds of tourism. It refers, first, to a particular approach to tourism development and planning and has its focus on attempts to create within a specific visitor destination greater community control over the nature, pace, and style of tourism development. While community may be conceptualized at different spatial levels (for example, international, as with the European Community; national, as with the UK, regional, as with Humberside in the UK, or the Auvergne in France), community tourism in this first sense finds its most common expression at the local level and refers to a relatively small spatial area. Thus, for example, the South Pembrokeshire Partnership for Action with Rural Communities booklet refers to 'the size of local communities' varying from 'around 2,000 in Narbeth, Saundersfoot and Kilgetty, to less than 300 in some villages' (SPARC, 1992, p. 2). Foster and Murphy (1991, p. 554) refer to the 'resort-retirement communities' of Parksville (population in 1986, 5,828 and Qualicum Beach (population in 1986, 3,410).

Second, 'community tourism' can refer to the collective provision of holidays for disadvantaged groups in a particular society. Community tourism in this sense can be seen as part of the wider concept, social tourism, which refers to the provision by the state and by voluntary bodies, of opportunities for disadvantaged groups to gain access to tourism. This wider concept includes both the social measures instigated by governments, and the measures taken by voluntary organizations, self-help groups, co-operatives, trade unions, youth groups, and churches. It is largely the activities of the latter groups that are defined here as 'community tourism', since they exhibit several features of the community approaches outlined and discussed in Part One of this book.

The two approaches to 'community tourism' introduced above will now be considered in greater detail.

Community tourism as local control over tourism development

Community tourism in this sense owes some of its origins to research that revealed wide-ranging impacts of tourism on host communities (Mathieson and Wall, 1982; Murphy, 1985) and to the growing realization that tourism, like other industries, could degrade the environment in which host communities had to live long after the visitors had departed. Many of these studies conceptualized community in spatial terms (as a village or an island) and were concerned with the physical/environmental, economic and socio-cultural impacts of tourism development particularly in areas in the 'pleasure periphery' (see, for example, Belisle and Hoy, 1980; Farrell, 1979; Hermans, 1981; Kemper, 1979; and Urbanowicz, 1977).

Numbers of studies acknowledged that 'communities' are made up of a variety of groups and that the impacts of tourism will be perceived differently by different groups. The impacts of tourism derive from a complex interaction in varied contexts and conditions of visitors and residents both made up of groups of differing social composition, with different interests and experiences. Various studies (see Murphy, 1985, pp. 120–6), have attempted to tease out the ways in which different groups within a host community experience tourism. Thus groups have been identified by socio-demographic characteristics, by place of residence and/or distance from the core tourist area, or on the basis of the degree of economic dependency on tourism. Conclusions varied according to the way in which groups were categorized. Studies dividing host communities according to socio-demographic features found little difference in the perceived impacts of tourism among the different social groups. Studies dividing communities into groups on the basis of place of residence and/or proximity to the core tourist area found that the perceived harmful impacts of tourism and hostility to visitors decreased as one moved from the core tourist area. Finally, when degree of economic dependency on tourism was considered, then, perhaps not surprisingly, the favourable disposition towards tourism increased with a group's economic dependency.

These studies are useful in that they indicate a range of different groups within any spatially defined community and show that the experience of tourism is by no means homogeneous. Problems of traffic congestion, parking, queuing, noise pollution, litter, vandalism, environmental degradation, health, and cultural decay, may loom larger in the view of those residents only marginally in touch with tourism and visitors compared with those residents who rely on tourism and visitors for a living. Those members of a community who have to compete daily with visitors for relatively scarce resources will, according to Doxey (1975), undergo changes in their approach to visitors as competition becomes more intense. Tolerance of visitors diminishes; resistance to further tourism development grows. The important feature of many of the impact studies is that they highlight the very real fears among certain members of host communities of changes that represent a loss of control over 'their' environment. As residents begin to perceive that their community identity (even if this may be a romanticized myth, Newby, 1979, pp. 154–98) is being changed (through, for example, an increase in antique shops, craft shops, cafés, restaurants, at the expense of the chemist, the butcher, the hardware shops) or is in danger of being lost, then there develops towards visitors an attitude at best ambivalent, at worst hostile.

This hostility can be expressed in a variety of ways. In Cornwall visitors are referred to as 'emmets' (ants), and in parts of the south of England as 'grockles', which are commercially worthless shellfish (Murphy, 1985, p. 31). Graffiti in parts of Scotland exhort the 'sassenachs' to go home. A Greek text on tourism in Crete states that 'tourists are the most dangerous of enemies because one needs them. There are various reasons why one cannot simply kill them as one did with enemies in earlier times. But one can remain silent' (quoted in Krippendorf, 1990, p. 44).

The dangers of arousing the hostility of residents may become even more pressing when those residents are a minority group within a particular society and when a particular identity is being constructed for this minority by those engaged in tourism development. Thus, for example, within the past few years it has become quite common for particular ethnic groups to be constructed as visitor attractions in some areas of the declining cities of the UK. Bradford, for example, has its 'curry trail' (Bates, 1986, p. 13) and Asian restaurants in the city have been marketed along with various aspects of the culture of people of Asian origin resident in the city (Urry, 1990, p. 144).

Generally, then, concern about tourism development will arise in relatively small spatial areas that have fairly clearly defined boundaries, where such areas act as visitor destinations and where tourism development is perceived as a threat to the *status quo* and to community identity. This concern will lead to demands from residents that they have more control over tourism development. This demand is likely to be complex, since communities will be made up of a variety of groups: business/commercial interests, which are likely to favour increased tourism development and visitor numbers; local politicians and local government officials, who may favour development because it is seen to increase employment prospects and bring wealth to an area; conservation and neighbourhood protection groups, who wish to preserve the environment and 'community identity'; and the passive and non-committed, who may gain indirectly from tourism, may perceive it as irrelevant to their lives, or may see no means of preventing 'them' from carrying out development (Krippendorf, 1990, pp.46–7).

The aims and concerns of the locally defined community may differ from the aims and concerns of the community defined regionally and nationally. But it is at the local level – the inner-city area, the rural village, the small town – that people have to deal with the effects of national and/or regional tourism development plans. It is at the local level where facilities are seen to be built, where land and other resources are allocated between competing users, and where wishes of permanent residents need to be accommodated as well as the needs of visitors.

An attempt to develop a model of tourism that incorporates different spatial levels of community has been made by Peter Murphy (1985). He suggests that there are different levels at which tourism development may be planned: national, regional, local (see Figure 6.1). At each of these levels there will be different degrees of public participation in the planning process, but it is at the local level where public participation should be at its greatest.

Within each of these spatially defined communities there will be different groups with different concerns: business, environmental, social, cultural. Each of these will be more or less well developed according to the carrying capacity of each host community. Carrying capacity refers to the maximum number of

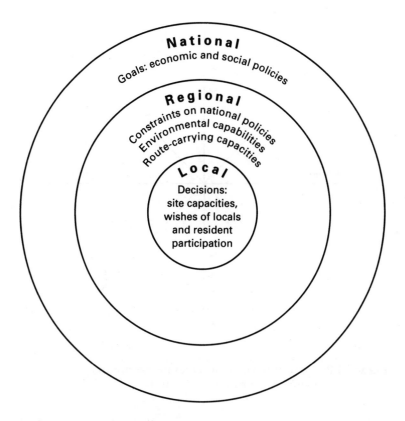

Figure 6.1 Levels of community
   Source: Murphy (1985), p. 168

people who can use a particular site without causing unacceptable changes in the economic, environmental and social sub-systems of the side, and without causing an unacceptable decline in the quality of the experience associated with the site gained by residents and visitors. (Mathieson and Wall, 1982, p. 21). A point of tourism balance will be achieved where all components can function without threat of unacceptable change. (See Figure 6.2). These components will exist at all three levels of community (Figure 6.3).

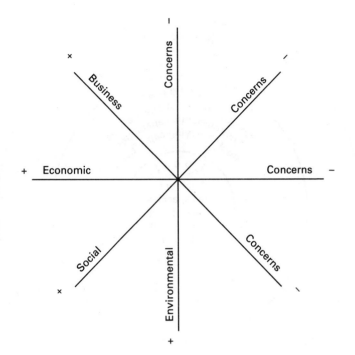

Figure 6.2 The tourism community: interest groups
Source: Murphy (1985), p. 168

Balanced tourism development will be best achieved by public participation in planning at all levels but particularly at the local level, because that, according to Murphy (1985, p. 172), 'is where the action takes place'. Murphy makes clear that there are problems with the notion of 'public participation', which is usually middle-class and environmentally orientated. Public participation does not tell us a great deal about the ways in which conflicting views on tourism development are dealt with and how consensus (which Murphy feels is more likely to exist than is usually believed) between groups is achieved. Issues of differential power are thus only hinted at by Murphy, in contrast to Krippendorf, who has no doubt that the dominant interest is likely to be economic (Krippendorf, 1990, p. 46).

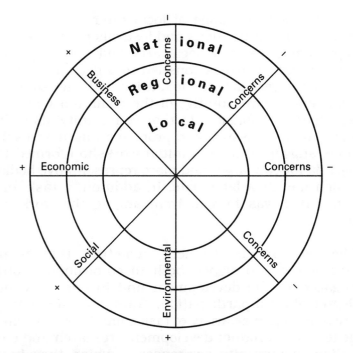

Figure 6.3 The tourism community
Source: Murphy (1985), p. 168

Community tourism in practice

One example of this first type of community tourism can be found in Murphy's own account of his part in tourism development in Greater Victoria, British Columbia, Canada (Murphy, 1985, pp. 177–8). A wish to reassess the structure and direction of the tourism industry seems to have originated with the industry itself, since the local chamber of commerce was a sponsor of the workshop set up to act as a forum for ideas about future developments in tourism. Some forty delegates, representing interest groups (attractions and festivals, community groups, economic support, government, hospitality, transportation and in-bound travel) were invited. Some of these groups included a wide range of local interests. Thus, for example, the attractions and festivals group included representatives from local arts and sports groups. The workshop discussions led to a generally agreed concern to restructure the tourism industry so that it was 'more representative of the community at large and more responsible to that community' (Murphy, 1985, p. 177). Issues and problems raised and solutions suggested at this initial workshop formed the agenda for two larger and more representative bodies, which met at a later date. In addition, a task force committee was formed from among the workshop delegates.

The tourism development structure that finally emerged was designed both to co-ordinate groups engaged in the development and to ensure a high degree of local participation. Thus interested groups are able to join a variety of task committees – revenue generation, product development, research and education, community awareness – which they judge appropriate for their particular contributions. These task committees then ensure that there is local participation through the development of a tourist product 'representative of the area and acceptable to the community' (Murphy, 1985, p. 177). A board of directors composed of members of the task committees and an executive committee derived from this board have to produce annual statements for local residents to evaluate the performance of the tourism industry and to indicate its contributions to the local economy.

A second illustration of community tourism can be seen in the Taf and Cleddau Rural Initiative (TCRI) and its successor, the South Pembrokeshire Partnership for Action with Rural Communities (SPARC) (SPARC, 1992). It should be emphasized that the schemes developed under this partnership are not solely concerned with tourism development, which is just one of a series of measures aimed at improving the social and environmental resources of the South Pembrokeshire area by creating tourism/agricultural/business training opportunities. The key point in the schemes is the focus on local people. Both TCRI and SPARC have their origins in the European Community Leader Programme, which aims to create rural development initiatives that will contribute to the reform of the Common Agricultural Policy. The programme is an initiative to encourage the diversification of the economies of predominantly rural areas. The emphasis is on what has been termed a 'bottom-up approach through which local rural communities can express their needs, enabling policy makers at national and community level to respond in a genuine partnership' (Ray McSharry, EC Commissioner for Agriculture quoted in SPARC, 1992, p. 1).

TCRI and SPARC seek to bring into the planning of future developments (including tourism) all sections of the small rural communities (with populations ranging from 300 to 2,000) as well as local government and development agencies. There is considerable emphasis on creating a consultative democratic structure 'to ensure maximum participation for the residents of each of the small communities ' (SPARC, 1992, p. 7). Each community has its own community association, to which all residents are entitled to belong. These associations – eighteen in August 1992, with a further twenty-four projected by the end of 1992 – appoint representatives to a consultative committee, which identifies how local needs can be linked into area-wide strategies, how these strategies can be achieved and who are the key partners. There is thus a move towards the multi-level approach to tourism planning advocated by Murphy and illustrated in his model of the tourism community (see Figure 6.3). Residents come together to identify their own local needs, a process intended to give everyone in a particular community an opportunity to think about local issues and to participate in discussion. Each community, through its community association, prepares an action plan based on the priorities identified at community association meetings. The action plan has to be fully endorsed 'by full consultation with the local community' (SPARC, 1992, p. 8) before implementation takes place.

Tourism is only one activity in an integrated approach to development. Other measures include encouraging developments in agriculture, small businesses, technical support and vocational training (SPARC, 1992, pp. 10–15). The underlying aim is to provide local people with an opportunity to help develop their own communities. It is perhaps too early to evaluate the extent to which these schemes have given local people in South Pembrokeshire some control over the pace and direction of change in the area. To a large extent this example of community tourism has its origin not in local concern for possible harmful effects of tourism but in governmental concern at the effects of changes likely to occur in rural areas as a result of reform of the Common Agricultural Policy. Nevertheless, SPARC and its predecessor, TCRI, do indicate a shift from the expert-knows-best approach to planning to an approach that seeks to bring as many people as possible into the planning process.

The initiative described in the previous paragraphs illustrates a paradox in that the schemes are intended to encourage grass-roots participation and control yet do not originate at grass roots but at governmental level. This contrasts sharply with the more radical community tourism exemplified in the village of Erschmatt in Valais in Switzerland. The Pro Erschmatt Society was a response to tourism development perceived as harmful. The Society's manifesto (Krippendorf, 1990, pp. 70–1) illustrates the concerns of many similar groups seeking greater control over tourism development:

'The Pro Erschmatt Society sees tourism as a possibility for development of the village. This can have its advantages and its drawbacks, it can work for the village and its population or against it. For this reason the Pro Erschmatt Society supports a healthy tourism adapted to local needs meeting the following criteria:

- It must benefit the population as a whole and not individual speculators.
- It must not abuse the environment – our capital – through speculation and thereby rob it of its recreational quality, but respect both the landscape and village architecture.
- It must take into account future generations and be based on medium- and long-term solutions, rather than on short term ones.
- It should allow the community to develop and should not impose a prohibitive infrastructural burden on it.
- It should not involve speculation leading to rocketing land prices, which make property too expensive for the local population.
- It should not lead to a sell-out of our country.
- It must not generate dead holiday villages, inhabited for only a few weeks in the year.
- It must be based on autonomous local decision-making, i.e. on equal participation of the local population in the planning and realization of tourist projects.
- It must create attractive jobs, take into account the local businesses and not waste building land.'

Community tourism as collective provision

The second meaning attached to the term community tourism is the collective provision of holidays for disadvantaged groups in a particular society. We would wish to distinguish here between 'community tourism' and 'social tourism'. Definitions of social tourism include the provision of holiday opportunities for low-income groups and those who on account of other restrictions (age, disability, family circumstances) are disenfranchised as far as the commercial sector of tourism is concerned. 'Social tourism' is a wider concept than 'community tourism', since the notion of the former includes both social measures by governments and the activities of a variety of voluntary organizations. A key feature of community tourism is that disadvantaged groups will make provision collectively for their members. This may or may not include support in the form of state subsidies. The state is not, however, central in this form of provision, and this feature distinguishes community tourism from social tourism, since the latter depends on collective provision made directly by the state to redistribute resources to particular disadvantaged groups.

We may then distinguish two broad strands of collective provision. One is where the state (central or local) provides financial assistance, either directly to families or to individuals in need. An extreme example of this kind of state intervention may be found in European countries from what was once the Soviet Union and Eastern Bloc, with centrally planned, command economies (Buckley and Witt, 1991; Deacon, 1992; Riordan, 1993; Jung, 1993), where, until recently at least, all tourism was controlled centrally by the state. Holidays were provided through the agency of the workplace or trade union to workers and their families. Since practically all domestic tourism in these countries was centrally controlled, it might therefore be considered as social tourism rather than community tourism. Where, however, the state works with voluntary organizations by giving them grants to build special holiday accommodation and facilities affordable to particular disadvantaged groups, then the boundaries between 'social tourism' (here seen as redistributive social policy by central government to enable particular groups to take part in tourism) and 'community tourism' (the initiatives taken by a variety of voluntary organizations to enable their members to have tourism opportunities) begin to blur. Thus, for example, in Denmark finance for tourism and leisure facilities is provided by the Ministry of Labour to the Dansk Folke Ferie (Danish People's Holidays) – a co-operative organization that runs holiday villages in Denmark, Italy, Norway, Spain, Portugal and Malta (Davidson, 1992, pp. 115–116.

This second strand of collective provision is, then, to be found in the activities of particular, groups often considered part of the voluntary sector in leisure. This movement, which comprises co-operative groups, self-help organizations, trade unions, churches and youth groups, is largely a feature of market liberal economies, since pressure groups, charities and voluntary organizations working for disadvantaged groups were until recently outlawed in the former command economies of the Soviet Union and East European states (Deacon, 1992; Riordan, 1993). Such organizations act either as not-for-profit tour operators, negotiating preferential transport and accommodation rates for their members, or as managing agents for accommodation, which the organization either owns or rents (Davidson, 1992, p. 113).

Community provision of holidays in Britain is sometimes traced back to 1841, with Thomas Cook's train trip offered to working people at considerably reduced prices. Other nineteenth-century antecedents may be found in organizations such as St Andrew's House and Club for Working-Boys, established in Soho, London, in 1866; in the Boys' Brigade; the Church Lads' Brigade; and later, at the turn of the century, the Boy Scouts and Girl Guides. All these organizations offered young people the chance of a holiday away from home at a time when holidays were the privilege of a few and family holidays the privilege of even fewer.

The Co-operative Movement was also important in developing community provision of holidays for adults. The Co-operative Holiday Association was formed in 1893 and developed a number of holiday camps and the Holiday Fellowship Organization. The Co-operative Wholesale Society and the Workers' Travel Association (founded in 1922) sponsored a travel organization, Travco Ltd, a non-profit-making company that aimed to provide camp holidays for individual workers of limited means, and family holidays (Ward and Hardy, 1986, p. 39). Other community provision may be found in trade-union organizations. The Derbyshire Housing Association, with funding from a holiday savings scheme, founded the miners' holiday camp at Skegness in Lincolnshire in 1939. The National and Local Government Officers' Association (NALGO) opened holiday centres in North Devon and Scarborough, North Yorkshire, in the 1930s. Local authorities also began to develop holiday camps and centres in the 1930s. The focus of concern was on the 70 per cent of the population unable to afford a holiday away from home (Ward and Hardy, 1986, p. 48).

Many of the early organizations were charitable and provided holidays and some sort of moral instruction/education mainly to children from families unable to afford a holiday. Other organizations developing in the latter half of the nineteenth and early part of the twentieth centuries aimed to provide holidays without the taint of charity or patronage and were of the self-help kind.

While many of the latter did for a time provide cheap holidays for low-income families, the ventures did not for long serve the groups for which they were intended. The problem for many manual workers remained low pay, and the Workers' Travel Association, for example, was by the end of the Second World war unable to provide holidays cheap enough to attract more than 10 per cent of its clientele from manual workers (Ward and Hardy, 1986, p. 43). With some noteworthy exceptions (the Derbyshire Miners' Holiday Centre, for example) many of the non-profit-making organizations have disappeared or have been turned into commercial enterprises operating under market principles. Some organizations such as the YHA and Holiday Fellowship, and uniformed organizations such as the Scouts and Guides, remain, but draw the bulk of their clientele from younger members usually from more affluent backgrounds. Other voluntary organizations, like MENCAP, offer holiday opportunities to those with a range of mental/physical impairments.

Funding of holidays is frequently complex, depending on state, voluntary and commercial sectors. Thus some MENCAP holidays are charged at the going commercial rate. Sometimes a local MENCAP Association makes the decision to donate funds (collected through flag days, coffee mornings, car boot sales) to the cost of holidays for local members, and clearly the extent of this depends very much on the available funds of the local association. Barnardo's similarly offers holiday opportunities to a variety of disadvantaged children. The extent of this voluntary group community tourism is not fully known, but the charity Holiday Care Service, created in 1981 by the English Tourist Board, is a valuable source of information on holiday provision for people whose age, disability, and family circumstances affect their choice of holiday (Davidson, 1992, p. 115). Similarly, little is known about the users of those organizations that do exist to provide low-cost holidays in the UK. The UK has no central funding agency to help those in need of a holiday, although social security departments do have permissive powers to help. Usually the social security departments work with a variety of groups from the commercial and voluntary sectors.

In Belgium, Denmark, France, Greece, Italy, Portugal and Spain there are a wide range of initiatives taken by voluntary groups and charities that make it reasonable to regard them as being active in community-tourism provision. Funding of holidays for low-income groups in several European countries is often covered by savings funds organized by trade unions. In Belgium and France, for example, there are trade-union savings schemes to which members contribute and from which repayments (usually a little larger than the deposits) are made at holiday times.

Switzerland uses the Swiss Travel Fund (REKA) as a means of funding holidays for low-income groups. The fund was founded in 1939 as a co-operative with the purpose of encouraging travel and holidays for those of limited financial means. REKA set out to provide both a method of saving for a holiday and an information service about low-priced holidays. The fund was developed by four groups: the travel and tourism industries, trade unions, employers, and co-operatives of various kinds. The fund's Board issues cheques to a variety of firms, service industries, and trade unions. Each organization sells the cheques to employees at a discount. Since commercially run hotels are usually too expensive for those on limited income, various approaches have been adopted to provide comfortable, non-expensive holiday accommodation. In some countries holiday centres have been created. In Switzerland REKA began to build its own centres in the 1950s, with accommodation designed for a variety of family groups. These centres, of which Leysin is perhaps the best known are equipped with golf courses, swimming pools, tennis courts, ski-ing facilities, children's playgrounds, and community buildings for bad weather. Accommodation is in individual apartments of one to four rooms with two to ten beds. All apartments contain a lounge-cum-kitchen and modern sanitation. Two of the centres provide an individual chalet for each family; others combine apartments in one building. In 1983 REKA owned six holiday centres and in 1982 accommodated 36,000 guests. A graded rental discount system is in operation and free holidays are offered to 300 families annually – more and more of these are to single mothers and their children (Teuscher, 1983).

It is worth noting, however, that the increased trend towards self-catering holidays does not always work towards the advantage of women in general, since such holidays are unlikely to reduce a woman's chores and she may well find that her 'holiday' consists of doing the same chores as at home but in a different location – with the added burden of stored up chores awaiting at the end of her holiday! (see Deem, 1992, p. 26.)

REKA is thus a much more elaborate scheme than a savings fund and sets out to channel funding into tourism. Holiday savings funds are not always able to ensure that the money withdrawn is so channelled. There is a similar disadvantage with social tourism measures such as the payment of holiday allowances and bonuses. There is no guarantee that the statutory increase in the length of paid annual holidays in France in the 1980s would lead to an increase in the proportion of the population going away on holiday (Hantrais, 1989, p. 83). In The Netherlands and the UK holiday bonuses are paid by some firms while in Belgium workers are paid a 'holiday wage', which is double the normal wage. Again there is no guarantee that the 'holiday wage' will be used for a holiday.

France has developed a special structure for tourism provision for those of limited means (Williams and Shaw, 1988, p. 193). This type of tourism, though relatively small-scale, is quite distinct from commercial tourism. Accommodation is paid for both by the state and by a variety of social organizations, including trade unions, employers and works committees, which often subsidize travel and run holiday homes for workers' children out of funds contributed by employers and the workers themselves. People on low incomes are able to use the accommodation through such channels as the social services and the trade unions. Accommodation is of a variety of collective types, including holiday camps, where individual bedrooms may be provided along with communal dineing-halls, lounges and a variety of entertainment and recreation facilities. The *Villages-Vacances-Familles*, founded in 1939 has some eighty establishments, ranging from the large village with full board to simpler gites. These holiday villages were the pioneers of what have become successful commercial holiday companies such as Club Mediterranean, which started life as a not-for-profit tourist organization (Davidson, 1992, p. 120).

The *Villages-Vacances-Familles* has attracted the attention of people in Quebec, Canada, where there is a similar wish to develop tourist structures for those of limited means (Moulin, 1983). Camping accommodation is also included in the French approach to provision for disadvantaged groups. In Greece some camp sites are operated by large industrial firms for the benefit of employees. In Greece also some 400,000 people – mainly those suffering some impairment, the unemployed and pensioners – have been helped to take a holiday (Williams and Shaw, 1988, p. 235).

In Denmark there are organizations to aid families and children who have difficulty taking a holiday. Young people's clubs (*Landsforeningen Ungdomsringen*) organize sports and other leisure activities and also supply family holiday accommodation (Davidson, 1992, p. 117). Pensioners' clubs, through the organization *Pensionnisternes Sanvirke,* negotiate with tour operators preferential rates for pensioners' holidays. Holidays for those who are visually or otherwise impaired are organized by *Dansk Blindesamfund* and *Landsforeningen af Vanfore* respectively (Davidson, 1992, p. 117).

In Belgium most of the holiday villages and holiday centres are owned and run by not-for-profit organizations such as the Christian Trade Union Movement, the Socialist Trade Union Movement and the Catholic Mutualist Movement. The holiday centres and villages are mainly located in the Ardennes mountains and on the coast, and provide a high standard of accommodation, family facilities and organized but non-compulsory activities. Facilities such as dining rooms, television lounges, and dormitory bedrooms are often shared, although this feature is becoming less important as the demand for more private facilities grows (Davidson, 1992, pp. 117–19).

In the UK there is no national policy for 'social tourism' and, with the election since 1979 of Conservative governments favouring self-help and liberal market principles, it seems likely that community tourism of the kind discussed in this section will become more important as self-help and voluntary groups increasingly seek to provide holidays for their members – either as a main function or as part of a more general service. These governments have helped to create a severe and protracted recession in the UK, leading to the fall in the income of some groups in society. Enforced early retirement, temporary contract work, and part-time work have increased the time available for leisure activities, while reducing the economic wherewithal to exercise choice to pursue many of them. Other groups – the physically and mentally impaired, pensioners, single parents – are similarly disadvantaged. With less money available to a considerable minority of people in the UK, low-priced, subsidized, good-quality holidays away from home will assume greater importance for a considerable number of people if a holiday is regarded as a social need.

How far social tourism will survive in the former communist regimes of Eastern Europe and the former Soviet Union is a matter of conjecture. The demise of the bureaucratic state collectivist system of welfare that accompanied the collapse of those regimes between 1989 and 1991 raises problems across a whole range of social policies, including the provision of holidays. In most of the regimes the state, through the place of work and/or trade unions did provide, though paternalistically, for those in established workplaces and with good work records, holiday homes, sanitoria, housing and other benefits.

With the move, at various speeds and with varying degrees of commitment and conviction, towards market type economies by these former communist regimes, it seems likely that all the disadvantages as well as the advantages of such economies (Breitenbach *et al.*, 1990, pp.15–18) will be produced in those countries. Undoubtedly, greater inequalities will appear, with widening and very visible gaps between the haves and the have-nots. There will be a series of problems facing social policy-makers in the period of transition from command to market economies (Deacon, 1992, pp. 8–9), not the least of which will be the continued heavy degree of reliance by some beneficiaries of state collectivist welfare on a range of social services, including holiday provision. To what extent former provision will lead to expectations for continuance and improvement of that provision depends on a variety of factors. It may be that the collective provision by the state of holidays for at least some sections of society is so strongly established that the demise of such provision will be resisted. On the other hand, the likelihood of there being fewer funds to finance a range of social policies may mean that social tourism is accorded low priority compared with housing, health, unemployment benefit and pensions (Jung, 1993, p. 202). It may well be therefore that voluntary sector led community tourism will grow in importance in former communist regimes as social tourism declines, thus paralleling what has happened in the West.

References

Bates, S. (1986) 'Curry country breaks with its image', *Daily Telegraph*, 7 October, p. 13.

Belisle, F. J. and Hoy, D. R. (1980) 'The perceived impact of tourism by residents: a case study in Santa Marta, Colombia', *Annals of Tourism Research*, Vol. 7, No. 1, pp. 83–101.

Bramham, P. *et al.* (1989) *Leisure and Urban Processes.* London: Routledge.

Bramham, P. *et al.* (eds) (1993) *Leisure Policies in Europe.* Wallingford: CAB International.

Breitenbach, H., Burden, T. and Coates, D. (1990) *Features of a Viable Socialism.* London: Harvester Wheatsheaf.

Buckley, P.J. and Witt, F. (1991) 'Tourism in the centrally planned economies of Europe', *Annals of Tourism Research*, Vol.17, No. 1, pp. 7–18.

Cater, E. (1987) 'Tourism in the Least Developed Countries', *Annals of Tourism Research*, Vol. 14, No. 2, pp. 202–26.

D'Amore, L.J. (1983) 'Guidelines in planning in harmony with the host community', in Murphy, P. (ed.) *Tourism in Canada: Selected issues and options, op. cit.*, pp. 135–59

Davidson, R. (1992) *Tourism in Europe.* Paris: Pitman Techniplus.

Deacon, R. (ed.) (1992) *The New Eastern Europe: Social Policy Past, Present and Future.* London: Sage.

Deem, R. (1992) 'The Sociology of Gender and Leisure in Britain – Past Progress and Future Prospects', *Leisure and Society*, Vol.15, No. 1, pp. 21–37.

Doxey, G.V. (1975) 'A causation theory of visitor-resident irritants – methodology and research inferences', The Impact of Tourism, Sixth Annual Conference Proceedings of the Travel Research Association, San Diego, pp. 195–8.

Farrell, B. (1979) 'Tourism's Human Conflicts: Cases from the Pacific', *Annals of Tourism Research*, Vol.6, No. 2, pp. 122–36.

Foster, D.M. and Murphy, P. (1991) 'Resort Cycle Revisited: The Retirement Connection', *Annals of Tourism Research*, Vol.18, No. 4, pp. 553–67.

Hantrais, L. (1989) 'Central Government Policy in France under the Socialist Administration', in Bramham, P. *et al.* (eds), *Leisure and Urban Processes, op. cit.*, pp. 68–89.

Haulot, A. (1983) The International Bureau of Social Tourism – Annual Report, *Annals of Tourism Research*, Vol. 10.

Hermans, D. (1981) 'The encounter of agriculture and tourism: A Catalan Case', *Annals of Tourism Research*, Vol.8, No. 3 pp. 462–79.

Jung, B. (1993) 'Elements of Leisure Policy in Post-War Poland', in Bramham, P. *et al.* (eds) (1993) *Leisure Policies in Europe, op. cit.*, pp. 189–210.

Kemper, R.V. (1979) 'Tourism in Taos and Patzcuaro: A Comparison of two approaches to Regional Development', *Annals of Tourism Research*, Vol.6, No. 1, pp. 91–110.

Krippendorf, J. (1990) *The Holiday Makers: Understanding the impact of leisure and travel*. London: Heinemann.

Lea, J. (1988) *Tourism and Development in the Third World*. London: Routledge.

Mathieson, A. and Wall, G. (1982) *Tourism: economic, physical and social impacts*. London: Longman.

Murphy, P. (ed.) (1983), *Tourism in Canada: Selected issues and options*, University of Victoria.

Murphy, P. (1985) *Tourism: A Community Approach*. London: Methuen.

Moulin, C. (1983) 'Social Tourism: Development and Prospects in Quebec', in Murphy, P. (ed.) *Tourism in Canada: Selected issues and options, op. cit.*, pp. 61–182.

Newby, H. (1979) *Green and Pleasant Land? Social Change in Rural England.* London: Wildwood House.

Pearce, D. (1986) Tourism Development. London: Longman.

Riordan, J. (1993) 'Leisure Policies in the Soviet Union', in Bramham, P. *et al.* (eds) *Leisure Policies in Europe, op. cit.*, pp. 211–30.

South Pembrokeshire Partnership for Action with Rural Communities (1992) *Partnership for Rural Prosperity: The TCRI and SPARC Initiatives.* Narbeth, Dyffed, Wales: SPARC.

Smith, V. (ed.) (1977) *Hosts and Guests: An Anthropology of Tourism,* Philadelphia: University of Pennsylvania Press.

Teuscher, H. (1983) 'Social tourism for all: the Swiss Travel Fund, *Tourism Management,* September, pp. 216–19.

Urbanowicz, C. F. (1977) 'Tourism in Tonga: Troubled Times', in Smith, V. (ed.), *Hosts and Guests: An Anthropology of Tourism, op. cit.*, pp. 84–92.

Urry, J. (1990) The Tourist Gaze. London: Sage.

Ward, C. and Hardy, D. (1986) Goodnight Campers! *The History of the Butlin's Holiday Camp.* London: Mansell.

Williams, A. M. and Shaw, G. (1988) *Tourism and Economic Development.* London: Belhaven Press.

Index